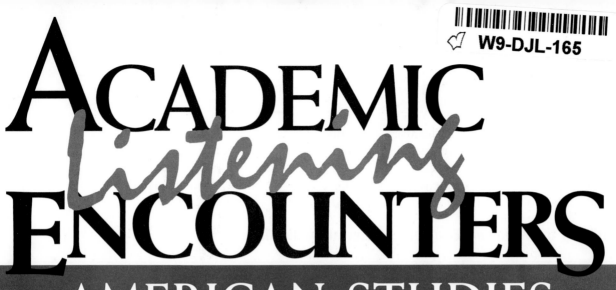

ACADEMIC *Listening* ENCOUNTERS

AMERICAN STUDIES

ACADEMIC ENCOUNTERS

The *Academic Encounters* series uses a sustained content approach to teach students the skills they need to be successful in academic courses. There are two books in the series for each content focus: an *Academic Encounters* title and an *Academic Listening Encounters* title. Please consult your catalog or contact your local sales representative for a current list of available titles.

Titles in the *Academic Encounters* series at publication:

Content Focus and Level	Components	Academic Encounters	Academic Listening Encounters
HUMAN BEHAVIOR High Intermediate to Low Advanced	Student's Book Teacher's Manual Class Audio Cassettes Class Audio CDs	978-0-521-47658-4 978-0-521-47660-7	978-0-521-60620-2 978-0-521-57820-2 978-0-521-57819-6 978-0-521-78357-6
LIFE IN SOCIETY Intermediate to High Intermediate	Student's Book Teacher's Manual Class Audio Cassettes Class Audio CDs	978-0-521-66616-9 978-0-521-66613-8	978-0-521-75483-5 978-0-521-75484-2 978-0-521-75485-9 978-0-521-75486-6
AMERICAN STUDIES Intermediate	Student's Book Teacher's Manual Class Audio CDs	978-0-521-67369-3 978-0-521-67370-9	978-0-521-68432-3 978-0-521-68434-7 978-0-521-68433-0

2-Book Sets are available at a discounted price. Each set includes one copy of the Student's Reading Book and one copy of the Student's Listening Book.

Academic Encounters:
Human Behavior 2-Book Set
978-0-521-89165-3

Academic Encounters:
Life in Society 2-Book Set
978-0-521-54670-6

Academic Encounters:
American Studies 2-Book Set
978-0-521-71013-8

ACADEMIC
Listening
ENCOUNTERS

AMERICAN STUDIES

Listening
Note Taking
Discussion

Kim Sanabria &
Carlos Sanabria

Intermediate

CAMBRIDGE UNIVERSITY PRESS
Cambridge, New York, Melbourne, Madrid, Cape Town, Singapore, São Paulo, Delhi

Cambridge University Press
32 Avenue of the Americas, New York, NY 10013-2473, USA

www.cambridge.org
Information on this title: www.cambridge.org/9780521684323

First published 2008

Printed in the United States of America

A catalog record for this book is available from the British Library

Library of Congress Cataloging-in-Publication Data

Sanabria, Kim, 1955–
   Academic listening encounters : American studies : listening, note taking,
discussion / Kim Sanabria & Carlos Sanabria.
      p. cm. – (Academic encounters)
   "Intermediate."
   Includes index.
   ISBN 978-0-521-68432-3 (Student's bk. : pbk. : w/audio cd) — ISBN
978-0-521-67370-9 — ISBN 978-0-521-68434-7 — ISBN 978-0-521-68433-0
   1. English language—Textbooks for foreign speakers. 2. English
language—Rhetoric—Problems, exercises, etc. 3. Listening—Problems,
exercises, etc. 4. Study skills—Problems, exercises, etc. 5. United
States—Civilization—Problems, exercises, etc. 6. Readers—United States.
I. Sanabria, Carlos, 1950– II. Title. III. Series.

   PE1128.S23 2008
   428.2—dc22

2007027760

ISBN 978-0-521-68432-3 paperback

Cover and book design: Adventure House, NYC
Text composition: Page Designs International
Audio production: Richard LePage & Associates

Contents

Plan of the Book

Unit 1 LAWS OF THE LAND
Chapter 1 The Foundations of Government

1 GETTING STARTED
(pages 2–3)

- Reading and Thinking About the Topic
- Previewing the Topic

2 AMERICAN VOICES
(pages 4–9)

BEFORE THE INTERVIEWS
- Building Background Knowledge and Vocabulary
- Examining Graphic Material

INTERVIEW WITH MANUEL, MARY, KELLY, AND RALPH: Reasons for voting or not voting
- Listening for Different Ways of Saying *Yes* and *No*

INTERVIEW WITH BOB: Issues that influence voter turnout
- Listening for Main Ideas in an Interview

AFTER THE INTERVIEWS
- Retelling What You Have Heard
- Sharing Your Opinion

3 IN YOUR OWN VOICE
(page 10)

- Sharing Your Knowledge
  Students use the board game "Find Someone Who . . ." as a tool to share their knowledge about the United States.

4 ACADEMIC LISTENING AND NOTE TAKING
(pages 11–15)

BEFORE THE LECTURE
- Listening for the Plan of a Lecture
- Note Taking: Using Information the Lecturer Puts on the Board

LECTURE: The Structure of the U.S. Federal Government (the Honorable Edward Sullivan)

Part One: The Three Branches of the U.S. Federal Government
- Guessing Vocabulary from Context
- Note Taking: Using Information the Lecturer Puts on the Board

Part Two: The System of Checks and Balances
- Guessing Vocabulary from Context
- Note Taking: Taking Good Lecture Notes

AFTER THE LECTURE
- Sharing Your Knowledge

Chapter 2 Constitutional Issues Today

1 GETTING STARTED (pages 16–18)	**2** AMERICAN VOICES (pages 19–23)	**3** IN YOUR OWN VOICE (page 24)	**4** ACADEMIC LISTENING AND NOTE TAKING (pages 25–32)

• Reading and Thinking About the Topic
ᏀᏋ • Understanding Numbers, Dates, and Time Expressions
	BEFORE THE INTERVIEWS
	  • Previewing the Topic
	
	INTERVIEW WITH MAGDA AND HANG: Important constitutional rights
	ᏀᏋ • Listening for Specific Information
	
	INTERVIEW WITH GLORIA: Another important right
	ᏀᏋ • Listening for Specific Information
	
	AFTER THE INTERVIEWS
	  • Understanding Humor About the Topic
		• Role Playing
		Working in small groups, students role play controversial situations. Then they share their opinions about the situations with the class.
			BEFORE THE LECTURE
			  • Predicting What You Will Hear
			ᏀᏋ • Note Taking: Listening for Main Ideas and Supporting Details
			
			LECTURE: The First Amendment (Professor Marcella Bencivenni)
			
			Part One: Overview of the First Amendment
			  • Guessing Vocabulary from Context
			ᏀᏋ • Note Taking: Using Symbols and Abbreviations
			
			Part Two: First Amendment Controversies
			  • Guessing Vocabulary from Context
			ᏀᏋ • Note Taking: Using a Map to Organize Your Notes
			
			AFTER THE LECTURE
			  • Conducting a Survey

Unit 2 A DIVERSE NATION

Chapter 3 The Origins of Diversity

1 GETTING STARTED (pages 34–36)	**2** AMERICAN VOICES (pages 37–40)	**3** IN YOUR OWN VOICE (pages 41–42)	**4** ACADEMIC LISTENING AND NOTE TAKING (pages 43–49)
• Reading and Thinking About the Topic • Building Background Knowledge 🎧 • Listening for Numerical Information	***BEFORE THE INTERVIEWS*** • Building Background Knowledge • Examining Graphic Material ***INTERVIEW WITH PATRICK:*** Immigration to the United States in the 1860s 🎧 • Answering True/False Questions ***INTERVIEW WITH EUNICE AND JOHN:*** Immigration to the United States in the 1900s 🎧 • Listening for Specific Information ***AFTER THE INTERVIEWS*** • Retelling What You Have Heard	• Conducting Research *Students research information about immigrants who entered the United States through Ellis Island in the late nineteenth and early twentieth centuries.* • Applying What You Have Learned *Students select one immigrant from a chart that gives basic facts about several immigrants. They create a story about that person's life and share their stories in groups or as a class.*	***BEFORE THE LECTURE*** • Building Background Knowledge and Vocabulary 🎧 • Note Taking: Listening for Transitional Phrases that Introduce Supporting Details ***LECTURE:*** Immigrants to America Face Prejudice but Make Lasting Contributions (Professor Gerald Meyer) ***Part One:*** Immigrants Face Prejudice • Guessing Vocabulary from Context 🎧 • Note Taking: Using Telegraphic Language ***Part Two:*** Immigrants Make Lasting Contributions • Guessing Vocabulary from Context 🎧 • Note Taking: Organizing Your Notes in Columns ***AFTER THE LECTURE*** • Answering Multiple Choice Questions

Chapter 4 Diversity in Today's United States

1 GETTING STARTED (pages 50–52)	**2 AMERICAN VOICES** (pages 53–56)	**3 IN YOUR OWN VOICE** (page 57)	**4 ACADEMIC LISTENING AND NOTE TAKING** (pages 58–64)
• Reading and Thinking About the Topic 🎧 • Listening for Percentages and Fractions	**BEFORE THE INTERVIEWS** • Sharing Your Opinion • Building Background Knowledge **INTERVIEW WITH AGUSTIN, NADEZHDA, AND CHAO:** Reasons for coming to the United States. 🎧 • Listening for Specific Information **INTERVIEW WITH ALVIN, MINSOO, AND ABDOUL-AZIZ:** Adapting to life in the United States 🎧 • Listening for Specific Information **AFTER THE INTERVIEWS** • Sharing Your Knowledge	• Giving an Oral Presentation *Working independently or in pairs, students choose a dish that was brought to America by an immigrant group but is now considered part of American cooking. They prepare and give a short oral presentation about the dish.*	**BEFORE THE LECTURE** • Previewing the Topic 🎧 • Note Taking: Listening for Definitions **LECTURE:** Recent Immigrants and Today's United States (Professor Betty Jordan) **Part One:** Metaphors for Describing American Society • Guessing Vocabulary from Context 🎧 • Note Taking: Using Numbers to Organize Your Notes **Part Two:** Transnationalism • Guessing Vocabulary from Context 🎧 • Note Taking: Using Bullets to Organize Your Notes **AFTER THE LECTURE** • Sharing Your Opinion

Unit 3 THE STRUGGLE FOR EQUALITY
Chapter 5 The Struggle Begins

1 GETTING STARTED (pages 66–69)	**2 AMERICAN VOICES** (pages 70–73)	**3 IN YOUR OWN VOICE** (page 74)	**4 ACADEMIC LISTENING AND NOTE TAKING** (pages 75–80)
• Reading and Thinking About the Topic 🎧 • Building Background Knowledge	***BEFORE THE INTERVIEWS*** • Building Background Knowledge ***INTERVIEW WITH CYNTHIA:*** Before the civil rights movement 🎧 • Listening for Answers to *Wh*-Questions ***INTERVIEW WITH HILDA:*** Before and after the women's movement 🎧 • Listening for Specific Information ***AFTER THE INTERVIEWS*** • Drawing Inferences	• Conducting Research *Working in groups, students do research about the life of an American who is famous for his or her contribution to the struggle for equality for African Americans or women.* • Giving an Oral Presentation *Each group prepares and gives a short presentation on the person it researched.* • Responding to Presentations *Students take notes during the presentations and write questions they would like to ask the presenters. After the presentations, students ask their questions, have the opportunity to make additional comments, and take notes on the new information they hear.*	***BEFORE THE LECTURE*** • Building Background Knowledge 🎧 • Note Taking: Listening for Guiding Questions **LECTURE:** The Civil Rights Movement and the Women's Movement (Professor Julia Smith) ***Part One:*** The Civil Rights Movement • Guessing Vocabulary from Context 🎧 • Note Taking: Creating Your Own Symbols and Abbreviations ***Part Two:*** The Women's Movement • Guessing Vocabulary from Context 🎧 • Note Taking: Organizing Your Notes in a Chart ***AFTER THE LECTURE*** • Reviewing Your Notes After a Lecture

Chapter 6 The Struggle Continues

1 GETTING STARTED (pages 81–82)	**2 AMERICAN VOICES** (pages 83–87)	**3 IN YOUR OWN VOICE** (pages 88–89)	**4 ACADEMIC LISTENING AND NOTE TAKING** (pages 90–96)
• Reading and Thinking About the Topic ᕦ • Listening for Specific Information	**BEFORE THE INTERVIEWS** • Building Background Knowledge **INTERVIEW WITH ROBIN:** Working with the blind ᕦ • Listening for Specific Information **INTERVIEW WITH JAIRO AND SANDY:** The struggle of two groups for equality ᕦ • Listening for Main Ideas **AFTER THE INTERVIEWS** • Sharing Your Opinion	• Thinking Critically About The Topic *Working in groups, students do one of three activities that explore stereotypes, tolerance, and discrimination.* • Giving an Oral Presentation *Each group gives a presentation about what they learned from the activity they chose.*	**BEFORE THE LECTURE** • Sharing Your Opinion ᕦ • Note Taking: Listening for Signal Words and Phrases **LECTURE:** Two Important Laws in the Struggle for Equality *(Mr. David Chachere)* **Part One:** The Age Discrimination in Employment Act • Guessing Vocabulary from Context ᕦ • Note Taking: Indenting **Part Two:** The Americans with Disabilities Act • Guessing Vocabulary from Context ᕦ • Note Taking: Using an Outline **AFTER THE LECTURE** • Using Your Notes to Make a Time Line

Unit 4 AMERICAN VALUES

Chapter 7 American Values From the Past

1 GETTING STARTED (pages 98–99)	**2 AMERICAN VOICES** (pages 100–104)	**3 IN YOUR OWN VOICE** (page 105)	**4 ACADEMIC LISTENING AND NOTE TAKING** (pages 106–111)
• Reading and Thinking About the Topic ♫ • Listening for Specific Information	*BEFORE THE INTERVIEWS* • Building Vocabulary *INTERVIEW WITH MARIELENA AND DAN:* Personal values ♫ • Answering True/False/Not Sure Questions *INTERVIEW WITH ANNE-MARIE AND LEILA:* Disagreeing with traditional values ♫ • Listening for Main Ideas *AFTER THE INTERVIEWS* • Sharing Your Opinion	• Giving an Oral Presentation *Students discuss the values represented by typical American sayings. Then partners select one of the sayings and make a short presentation about why they agree or disagree with it. Afterwards, the class makes comments and asks questions of the presenters.*	*BEFORE THE LECTURE* • Sharing Your Knowledge ♫ • Note Taking: Listening for Key Words *LECTURE:* Three American Folk Heroes (Professor Peter Roman) *Part One:* Three American Folk Heroes • Guessing Vocabulary from Context ♫ • Note Taking: Clarifying Your Notes *Part Two:* Questions and Answers • Guessing Vocabulary from Context ♫ • Note Taking: Taking Notes on Questions and Answers *AFTER THE LECTURE* • Sharing Your Opinion

Chapter 8 American Values Today

1 GETTING STARTED (pages 112–114)	**2** AMERICAN VOICES (pages 115–119)	**3** IN YOUR OWN VOICE (pages 120–121)	**4** ACADEMIC LISTENING AND NOTE TAKING (pages 122–128)
• Reading and Thinking About the Topic • Sharing your Knowledge ☊ • Listening for Specific Information	**BEFORE THE INTERVIEWS** • Sharing your Opinion **INTERVIEW WITH ROSIANE, DAN-EL, AND CHRISTINE:** Differences in values between parents and children ☊ • Drawing Inferences **INTERVIEW WITH SANDY:** Values in the workplace ☊ • Listening for Specific Information • Role Playing **AFTER THE INTERVIEWS** • Sharing Your Opinion	• Conducting a Survey *Students conduct a short survey to find out what people think is important in a job. Then they share their findings in groups.*	**BEFORE THE LECTURE** • Building Background Knowledge ☊ • Note Taking: Listening for General Statements **LECTURE:** Conservative and Liberal Values in American Politics (Professor Jason Rose) **Part One:** Conservative and Liberal Values • Guessing Vocabulary from Context ☊ • Note Taking: Taking Notes in a Point-by-Point Format **Part Two:** Values and Political Parties • Guessing Vocabulary from Context ☊ • Note Taking: Using a Handout to Help You Take Notes **AFTER THE LECTURE** • Sharing Your Opinion

Chapter 10 Global Transformations

Authors' Acknowledgments

We offer our sincere gratitude to Bernard Seal, Academic Encounters series editor, who is a fountain of support and inspiration; Lida Baker, the editor who graciously put us through many paces in the preparation of the manuscript; and Kathleen O'Reilly, a demanding Senior Development Editor whose eye for balance and detail was our constant guide. Jessica Williams, author of the companion text, *Academic Encounters: American Studies*, also provided us with good suggestions and moral support. Next, we want to extend thanks to others who have worked hard on this project including Cindee Howard, Senior Project Editor; Leslie DeJesus, Editorial Assistant; Don Williams, a master compositor; Richard LePage, our talented audio producer; and the teachers who reviewed the book at various stages of development: Nancy Braiman, Byron-Bergen High School; Joy Campbell, Michigan State University; Susan Lafond, Guilderland High School; Tim McDaniel, Green River Community College; Juan Gabriel Garduño Moreno, Universidad Autónoma Metropolitana Xochimilco; Anthony James Rosenberg, Centro Universitário Ibero-Americano; Pelly Shaw, American University of Sharjah; Heshim Song, Seokyeong University; and Richmond Stroupe, Soka University. We are honored to have benefited from everyone's attentive concern.

Finally, we would like to acknowledge the many individuals who appear on these pages, both lecturers and interviewees, who shared so much of their life experiences with us and have made this book real – and to say a big thank-you to our wonderful daughter and son.

Kim Sanabria & Carlos Sanabria

Introduction

To the Instructor

ABOUT THIS BOOK

Academic Listening Encounters: American Studies is a listening, note-taking, and discussion text based on content taught in American history and culture courses in high schools, colleges, and universities in the United States.* The book aims to give a broad overview of the United States from its founding to the present, while presenting students with topics relevant to their lives today. The listening, note-taking, and discussion tasks help students develop the skills they need for study in any academic discipline.

The complete audio program for this book, which contains the recorded material for the listening and note-taking tasks, is available on Class Audio CDs. A Student Audio CD of the academic lectures, which are an important part of the audio program, is included in the back of each Student's Book to provide students with additional listening practice.

Correlation with Standards

Academic Listening Encounters: American Studies introduces students to many of the topics and skills in the United States secondary school standards for American history and social studies. For more information about the standards, go to www.cambridge.org/us/esl/academicencounters.

TOEFL® iBT Skills

Many of the tasks in *Academic Listening Encounters: American Studies* (as well as those in all *Academic Listening Encounters* books) teach academic skills tested on the TOEFL® iBT test. For a complete list of the tasks taught, see the Task Index on page 163.

ABOUT THE ACADEMIC ENCOUNTERS SERIES

This content-based series is for students who need to improve their academic skills for further study. The series consists of *Academic Encounters* books that help students improve their reading, study skills, and writing, and *Academic Listening Encounters* books that concentrate on listening, note-taking, and discussion skills. The reading books and listening books are published in pairs, and each pair of books focuses on a subject commonly taught in academic courses: *Academic Encounters: American Studies* and *Academic Listening Encounters: American Studies* focus on American history and culture; *Academic Encounters: Life in Society* and *Academic Listening Encounters: Life in Society* focus on

---

* Although the term *Americas* can be used to refer to all of North and South America, America is often used to refer to the United States of America alone. The phrase "American Studies" in the title reflects that usage. American Studies is an academic discipline with a focus similar to that of this book: United States history and culture.

sociology; and *Academic Encounters: Human Behavior* and *Academic Listening Encounters: Human Behavior* focus on psychology and human communications. A reading book and a listening book with the same content focus may be used together to teach a complete four-skills course in English for Academic Purposes.

ACADEMIC LISTENING ENCOUNTERS LISTENING, NOTE-TAKING, AND DISCUSSION BOOKS

The approach

Focusing on a particular academic discipline allows students to gain a sustained experience with one field and encounter concepts and terminology that overlap and grow more complex. It provides students with a realistic sense of studying in an academic course. As language and concepts recur and as students' skills develop, they begin to gain confidence until they feel that they have enough background in the content focus area to take a course in that subject (e.g., American history) to fulfill part of their general education requirements.

The format

Each book consists of five units on different aspects of the discipline. Each unit is divided into two chapters. Each chapter has four sections and includes an introductory listening exercise, a selection of informal interviews, an opportunity for students to conduct and present a topic-related project, and a two-part academic lecture. A variety of listening, note-taking, and discussion tasks accompany the listening material. Chapters are structured to maximize students' comprehension of the chapter topic. Vocabulary and ideas are recycled through the four sections of each chapter, and recur in later chapters as students move from listening to discussion, and from informal to academic discourse.

A chapter-by-chapter Plan of the Book appears in the front of the book, and an alphabetized Task Index is at the back of the book.

The audio program

The heart of all *Academic Listening Encounters* books is the authentic listening material. The audio program for each chapter includes a warm-up listening exercise designed to introduce the chapter topic, informal interviews that explore a particular aspect of the topic, and a two-part academic lecture on another aspect of the topic. Each of these three types of listening experiences exposes students to a different style of discourse, while recycling vocabulary and concepts.

Tasks that involve listening to the audio material have an earphones icon 🎧 next to the title. A second symbol ▶ PLAY indicates the exact point within the task when the audio material should be played.

The complete audio program is available in a set of three Class Audio CDs. A Student Audio CD of the academic lectures is included in the back of each Student's Book to provide students with additional listening practice.

The skills

The three main skills developed in *Academic Listening Encounters* books are listening, note taking, and discussion. Listening is a critical area because, unlike text on a page, spoken words are difficult to review. In addition to the content and vocabulary students hear, they are challenged by different voices, speeds of delivery, and other features of oral discourse. Tasks in the *Academic Listening Encounters* books guide students in techniques for improving their listening comprehension. However, these tasks also develop note-taking skills in a structured format that teaches students to write down what they hear in ways that will make it easier to retrieve the information. After the listening and note-taking practice, students discuss what they have heard, voice their opinions, compare their experiences, and articulate and exchange viewpoints with other class members, thus making the material their own. Additionally, each chapter gives students the opportunity to work on a project related to the topic, such as conducting a survey or undertaking research, and teaches them the skills necessary to present their findings.

Task commentary boxes

Whenever a task type occurs for the first time in the book, it is headed by a colored commentary box that explains what skill is being practiced and why it is important. When the task occurs again later in the book, it may be accompanied by another commentary box, either as a reminder or to present new information about the skill. At the back of the book, there is an alphabetized index of all the tasks. Page references in boldface indicate tasks that are headed by commentary boxes.

Opportunities for student interaction

Many of the tasks in *Academic Listening Encounters* are divided into steps. Some of these steps are to be done by the student working alone, others by students in pairs or in small groups, and still others by the teacher with the whole class. To make the books as lively as possible, student interaction has been built into most activities. Thus, although the books focus on listening and note-taking skills, discussion is fundamental to each chapter. Students often work collaboratively and frequently compare answers in pairs or small groups.

Order of units

In terms of topics and vocabulary, the order of the units is regarded as optimal. In addition, tasks do increase in complexity so that, for example, a note-taking task later in the book may draw upon information that has been included in an earlier unit. Teachers who want to use the material out of order may, however, consult the Plan of the Book at the front of the book or the Task Index at the back of the book to see what information has been presented in earlier units.

Course length

Each chapter of a Listening, Note-Taking, and Discussion book is divided into four sections and represents approximately 7–11 hours of classroom material. Thus, with a 90-minute daily class, a teacher could complete all 10 chapters in a 10-week course. For use with a shorter course, a teacher could omit chapters or activities within chapters. The material could also be expanded with the use of guest speakers, debates, movies, and other authentic audio material (see the Teacher's Manual for specific suggestions).

CHAPTER FORMAT

1 Getting Started (approximately 1 hour of class time)

This section contains a short reading task and a listening task. The reading is designed to activate students' prior knowledge about the topic, provide them with general concepts and vocabulary, and stimulate their interest. Comprehension and discussion questions elicit their engagement in the topic.

The listening task in this section is determined by the chapter content and involves one of a variety of responses. The task may require students to complete a chart, do a matching exercise, or listen for specific information. The task provides skill-building practice and also gives students listening warm-up on the chapter topic.

2 American Voices (approximately 2–3½ hours of class time)

This section contains informal audio interviews on issues related to the chapter. It is divided into three subsections:

Before the Interviews (approximately ½ hour)

This subsection contains a prelistening task that calls on students to predict the content of the interview or share what they already know about the topic from their personal experience. Allow enough time with this task for all students to contribute. The more they invest in the topic at this point, the more they will get out of the interviews.

Interviews (approximately 1–2 hours)

In this subsection, students listen to interviews related to the topic of the chapter. Most of the interviewees are native speakers of English, but voices of immigrants to the United States also enrich the discussions. The interviewees are of different ages and ethnic and social backgrounds, allowing students to gain exposure to the rich and diverse reality of speakers of English. The interviews are divided into two parts to facilitate comprehension; each part can include from one to three interviewees.

Each interview segment begins with a boxed vocabulary preview that glosses words and phrases the student may not know. The vocabulary is given in the context in which students will hear it. Reading this vocabulary aloud and exploring its meaning within the context will facilitate students' comprehension.

After each vocabulary preview, students are given the opportunity to scan the upcoming task. Then they listen to the interview and go on to complete the particular task, which might include listening for main ideas or details, drawing inferences, or taking notes on the material to retell what they have heard. This approach provides a framework for listening, teaches basic listening skills, and allows students to demonstrate their understanding of the interviews.

After the Interviews (approximately ½–1 hour)

In this subsection, students explore the topic more deeply through examining graphic material related to the content of the interviews, thinking critically about what they have heard, or sharing their perspective. Most of the tasks in this section are for pairs or small groups and allow for informal feedback from every student.

3 In Your Own Voice (approximately 1½–2½ hours of class time)

This section continues to build on the chapter topic and is designed to give students the opportunity to take creative control of the topic at hand. Specific tasks, brief descriptions of which are provided in the Plan of the Book, are determined by the chapter content. They may include:

- *Personalizing the content,* in which students talk with partners or in small groups, sharing their experiences and supporting their points of view
- *Gathering data,* in which students conduct surveys or interviews of classmates or people outside the class, or in which they undertake small research projects
- *Presenting data,* in which students organize their data and present it individually or in small groups

4 Academic Listening and Note Taking (approximately 2½–4 hours of class time)

This section contains a formal, recorded, academic lecture related to the topic of the chapter. It is divided into three subsections:

Before the Lecture (1–1½ hours)

The first task of this subsection asks students to predict the content of the lecture, explore what they already know about the topic, or build their background knowledge and vocabulary by doing a task related to a brief reading, syllabus, or other written entry. As with Before the Interview, this section promotes the students' investment in the topic.

Each chapter then proceeds to an academic note-taking skill, determined by the language of the lecture itself and sequenced to build upon skills studied in previous chapters. The skill is explained in a task commentary box, and the listening task is designed to practice it. The recorded material used for the task is drawn from the lecture.

Lecture (1–1½ hours)

In this subsection, students hear the lecture itself. To facilitate comprehension, all lectures are divided into two parts.

Each lecture part begins with a matching or multiple choice vocabulary task to prepare students for the language they will encounter in the lecture and help them develop their ability to guess meaning from context. Potentially unfamiliar words and phrases are given in the context in which they will be used in the lecture. Reading the items aloud, studying their pronunciation, and exploring their use and meaning will prepare students for hearing them in the lecture.

Following the vocabulary task, students preview a comprehension task designed to provide a framework for their listening and note taking. The task may involve completing a summary or outline or answering comprehension questions. The task may recycle the note-taking skill taught before the lecture or add a related skill. Students are instructed to take notes during each part of the lecture, and then use their notes to complete the lecture comprehension task. Previewing the task will enable students to answer the questions in a more confident and focused manner.

After the Lecture (½–1 hour)

This subsection invites students to share their perspectives through discussion questions that allow them to analyze the chapter content more critically. It may also present additional information or ask students to apply what they have learned.

GENERAL TEACHING GUIDELINES

1. Replay recorded excerpts as many times as you think will benefit the majority of students.
2. Encourage students to gain additional listening practice by listening to the chapter lectures that are on the audio CD in the back of the Student's Book. Depending on the level of the class, you may want students to listen either before or after you have played the lecture for them in class.
3. Homework assignments can include thinking and writing about discussion questions, doing Internet research, and preparing and rehearsing presentations.
4. If possible, pair students from different cultural and linguistic backgrounds.
5. Depending on your students' level of interest and time constraints, you may want to pick and choose from the activities in After the Interview and After the Lecture. It is not necessary to do all of them.
6. To some extent, the course material builds upon itself. Skills are recycled (see the Plan of the Book) and the level of exercises increases slightly in difficulty. However, it is not necessary to do the units in order, and you can skip ones that are less appropriate for your students.
7. If you prefer to read the script of a lecture rather than play the recording, try to match the natural pace of the recorded lectures.
8. Refer to the Teacher's Manual for teaching suggestions, answer keys, the listening script, and lecture quizzes and answers.

To the Student

Improving your language skills is a journey of discovery, allowing you to learn new things about other people and yourself. *Academic Listening Encounters: American Studies* can help you along this path. The material in this book is taken from the discipline of American Studies, which combines the history and culture of the United States. The topics in this book have been chosen for their high interest and relevance to American life today.

Active involvement is at the heart of any type of learning, so you should use this book as a context for your own experience. In this book you may find ideas that surprise you, concepts that catch your attention, or stories that make you want to share an experience in your own life with your classmates.

You will also learn the skills you need to be successful in an academic classroom.

You will learn:
- what to listen for in casual situations such as informal interviews
- what to listen for in academic lectures
- note-taking techniques
- how to use your notes to prepare for tests
- ways to think critically about what you have heard
- ways to discuss what you have heard

Use the opportunity to develop your listening skills while you listen to others contribute their voices to the class discussion. Then take your turn at sharing your own impressions and experiences. If you are shy about speaking, consider that discussion is an art that we all continue to improve throughout our lives, and always remember that other people will be enriched by what you have to say.

Good luck with your academic studies!

Kim Sanabria & Carlos Sanabria

THE UNITED STATES OF AMERICA

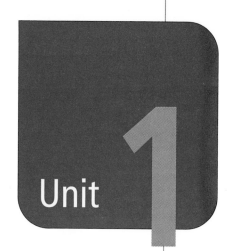

Unit 1

Laws of the Land

"The Adoption of the Constitution," J.B. Stearns

In this unit, you will learn about the U.S. Constitution, the document that is the basis for the structure of the government of the United States. Chapter 1 focuses on the basic organization of the government and the history behind it. You will hear people of various ages and backgrounds speaking about why they do or do not vote and a lecture about the three branches of the U.S. government. In Chapter 2, you will learn about the Bill of Rights, which is the name given to the first 10 amendments, or changes, that were added to the Constitution after it was adopted in 1789. The interviews in Chapter 2 are about topics in the Constitution that often create disagreement among Americans. The lecture discusses the First Amendment, which guarantees important rights and freedoms to all Americans.

Chapter 1

The Foundations of Government

The Great Seal of the United States

1 GETTING STARTED

In this section, you will read about the foundations, or beginnings, of the United States government. You will also listen to a conversation about some important symbols that are found on the Great Seal of the United States. The seal is used on passports and other official government documents.

READING AND THINKING ABOUT THE TOPIC

Reading and thinking about a topic before you hear about it helps you review what you already know and get ready to listen to new information.

1 | Read the following passage.

The United States has had its system of government for more than 200 years. This system is based on a number of important principles.

First, the United States is a *republic*. This means that the head of the government is a President, not a king or queen. Second, the United States is a *democracy*. In other words, the power to make decisions belongs to representatives chosen by the people. Citizens of the United States have the right to vote for the President and for their other representatives in regular, free elections. *Federalism* is another important principle. It means that there are different levels of government: the federal (national) level, the state level, and the local level.

According to the Constitution, the federal government has three branches, called legislative (the Congress), executive (the President and Vice President), and judicial (the courts). Under a system of *checks and balances*, each branch has separate responsibilities, but the branches work together to govern the country. The men who wrote the Constitution designed the government this way so that no branch would have too much power.

2 | Answer the following questions according to the information in the passage:

 1 What are three principles that form the foundation of the United States government?

 2 What important right do citizens of the United States have?

 3 What is the purpose of the system of checks and balances?

3 | Read these questions and share your responses with a partner:

 1 How is the U.S. government similar to or different from other governments that you know about?

 2 In the United States, people vote for their President and their representatives. How are leaders chosen in other countries you know about?

⌒ PREVIEWING THE TOPIC

Previewing means looking at pictures or other visual materials, skimming handouts your teacher gives you, or perhaps reviewing key vocabulary about a topic before listening to people talk about it. Doing these things will prepare you for listening and will improve your ability to understand what you hear.

1 | You will hear a conversation about some symbols that appear on the back of a U.S. one-dollar bill. Look at the numbered symbols in this picture. Find the same symbols in the larger picture on page 2. What are they? Can you guess what each one represents?

2 | Now listen to the conversation and write the number of each symbol next to what it represents in the list below. ▶ **PLAY**

 _____ **a** The national symbol of the United States

 _____ **b** The 13 original states of the United States

 _____ **c** The fact that America is a country with a strong foundation

 _____ **d** The fact that the United States is one nation made of many states and many people

 _____ **e** The year that the United States became independent from Britain

2 AMERICAN VOICES: Manuel, Mary, Kelly, Ralph, and Bob

In this section, you will hear five people of different ages and backgrounds talk about voting. First you will hear Manuel, Mary, Kelly, and Ralph discuss why they do or do not vote. Then you will hear Bob talking about some issues that influence voter turnout (the percentage of people who vote in an election).

BEFORE THE INTERVIEWS

BUILDING BACKGROUND KNOWLEDGE AND VOCABULARY

Learning background information and vocabulary related to a topic can help you understand the topic better when you listen to people talking about it.

Americans voting on Election Day

1 | The following words and expressions are used to talk about voting. Work in a small group and discuss the meanings of the words. Use a dictionary if necessary.

candidate	issue	runs for office
compulsory	(political) party	vote
election(s)	the polls	

2 | Read this passage about voting in the United States. Use vocabulary from step 1 to fill in the blanks. Then check your answers with the members of your group.

All U.S. citizens have the right to _____ in national _____ at the age of 18. Voting is also called "going to _____." In the United States, voting is voluntary, not _____. Voters choose the _____ they support and vote for that person on Election Day.

Voters may make their decision for different reasons. One reason might be that they support one _____ – for example, Democratic or Republican. Another reason might be that they feel strongly about a particular _____ such as education, crime, or foreign policy, and they want to express their opinion by electing the candidate who agrees with them.

Most of the time, there are only two main candidates in U.S. elections – a Democrat and a Republican. Occasionally, a third candidate _____, but third-party candidates almost never win in the United States.

EXAMINING GRAPHIC MATERIAL

Graphic material refers to information that is presented visually in graphs, diagrams, charts, and tables. Graphs show different kinds of numerical information about a topic, including facts, trends (changes over time), and comparisons. For example, a graph about voting might show:

- **a fact**: the number of people or percentage of the population that votes
- **a trend**: an increase or decrease in the number of people who vote
- **a comparison**: the difference in voting practices between (year) and (year)

The graph below shows voter turnout between 1940 and 2004. Work with a partner and study the graph. Then discuss the questions that follow.

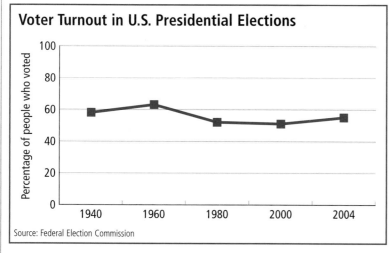

Voter Turnout in U.S. Presidential Elections

Source: Federal Election Commission

1 Does this graph show some facts, a trend, a comparison, or all of these?
2 In what year was voter turnout the highest?
3 What happened between 1960 and 1980?
4 Approximately what percentage of people voted in 2004?
5 Does any information in the graph surprise you? Why or why not?

INTERVIEW WITH MANUEL, MARY, KELLY, AND RALPH: Reasons for voting or not voting

Here are some words and phrases from the interview printed in **bold** and given in the context in which you will hear them. They are followed by definitions.

It's still not **convenient** for a lot of people: *easy to do*

I just **couldn't make it**: *couldn't do what I had planned*

It's important . . . to vote because . . . it gives you **a voice**: *an opportunity to express yourself*

When you vote, you get to say . . . who can help more in **dealing with** the country's problems: *trying to solve*

I think voting is a **civic duty**: *responsibility of a citizen*

I read that in 34 countries, voting is **an obligation**: *something you must do*

I don't trust most politicians: *I think [they] are not honest*

⌬ LISTENING FOR DIFFERENT WAYS OF SAYING *YES* AND *NO*

Speakers don't always answer yes/no questions with those exact words. Here are some other ways of saying *yes* and *no*.

Yes:	Sure	No:	I would have, but . . .
	Definitely		Well, not usually
	Absolutely		Not really
	Yeah (informal)		Nope/Nah (informal)

1 | Work with a partner and think of ways to say yes and no that are different from the ones in the box above. Write them in the margins next to the box.

2 | Look at the photographs of the interviewees. The interviewer asks them: "Do you vote?" Listen and circle *Y* (yes) or *N* (no). ▶ PLAY

Manuel Y N

Mary Y N

Kelly Y N

Ralph Y N

3 Listen again. Match the speakers with their reasons for voting or not voting. ▶ **PLAY**

_____ **1** Manuel   **a** Voting gives you a voice.

_____ **2** Mary   **b** There is no holiday on Election Day.

_____ **3** Kelly   **c** You can't trust most politicians.

_____ **4** Ralph   **d** Voting is a civic duty.

4 Work with a partner and compare answers. Then discuss whether you agree or disagree with the speakers' reasons for voting or not voting.

INTERVIEW WITH BOB: *Issues that influence voter turnout*

Bob

Here are some words and phrases from the interview with Bob printed in **bold** and given in the context in which you will hear them. They are followed by definitions.

Some people don't think [voting] will **make any difference**: *have any effect*

A lot of people feel . . . their vote isn't **meaningful**: *significant, important*

[The first issue] is **immigration**: *moving to a new country to live*

We need to elect **representatives** who share our concerns: *officials that voters elect to serve in government*

⌒ LISTENING FOR MAIN IDEAS IN AN INTERVIEW

Main ideas are the important points that a speaker wants to make. In an interview, you have to listen carefully to the questions as well as the answers in order to understand the main ideas. For example:

Interviewer: What are some issues that are important to you?

Bob: Hmmm. Let's see. . . . Well . . . one is immigration.

One of Bob's main ideas is: *Immigration is an important issue.*

1 | The following questions are about the main ideas in the interview with Bob. Read the questions before you listen.

1 According to Bob, why do so few Americans vote? Check (✔) all the reasons you hear.

_____ **a** People are too busy.

_____ **b** There is no legal requirement to vote.

_____ **c** People don't think their vote will make any difference.

_____ **d** The political parties often disagree.

_____ **e** The parties are very similar.

2 Does Bob think it is important to vote? Check (✔) one.

_____ **a** Yes

_____ **b** No

_____ **c** Not sure

3 Which issues does Bob think are important today? Check (✔) all the issues you hear.

_____ **a** education

_____ **b** equality

_____ **c** crime

_____ **d** health care

_____ **e** homelessness

_____ **f** immigration

_____ **g** the environment

2 | Now listen to the interview. Check (✔) all of Bob's responses to the questions.
▶ PLAY

3 | Work with a partner and compare answers. Then discuss the following question: Of the issues listed above, which ones are important to you also? Why?

AFTER THE INTERVIEWS

RETELLING WHAT YOU HAVE HEARD

Using your own words to retell what you have heard helps you check your understanding and review important ideas and vocabulary.

Work in groups of five students. Each member of the group should play the role of one of the speakers from the interviews (Manuel, Mary, Kelly, Ralph, or Bob). Take turns explaining why you do or do not vote and asking your classmates questions about their reasons.

Example:

My name is Kelly, and I think it's important to vote because . . .

SHARING YOUR OPINION

Sharing your opinion about information you have heard helps you review the material and learn about other people's ideas.

You can use the following expressions to introduce your ideas:

I think . . .
I believe . . .
In my opinion . . .
In my view . . .
I agree (with X) that . . .
I disagree (with Y) because . . .

Work in small groups and discuss the questions below. Use expressions from the box above to express your opinion and to respond to your classmates' opinions.

1 Do you believe voting should be compulsory?

2 What are three issues that are important to you? Why do you care about them?

3 Which characteristic do you think is most important in an elected representative? Choose a characteristic from the list below or add your own. Explain why you think it is important.

honesty	good speaking skills
good administrative skills	good looks
intelligence	leadership skills
love of one's country	strong religious beliefs

3 IN YOUR OWN VOICE

In this section, you and your classmates will play a game in which you share your knowledge about the United States.

SHARING YOUR KNOWLEDGE

Sharing your knowledge with your classmates makes you more aware of what you know about a topic and lets you learn new information.

1 | Walk around the classroom and ask your classmates for the answers necessary to fill in the boxes below. In the appropriate box, write the answer and the name of the classmate who gave it to you. If you know an answer, share your information with your classmates.

Find someone who . . .		
1 can name the capital of the United States.	2 knows the number of states in the United States today.	3 knows the name of the national anthem (national song).
4 can describe the American flag.	5 knows when America declared its independence.	6 knows where the U.S. President lives.
7 can name two U.S. national holidays (not religious holidays).	8 can name one of the Founding Fathers (eighteenth-century leaders) of the United States.	9 can name three current or recent U.S. government leaders.

2 | Go over the answers as a class. Share any additional information you know about each item with your classmates. (You can check your answers at the bottom of page 11.)

4 ACADEMIC LISTENING AND NOTE TAKING: The Structure of the U.S. Federal Government

In this section, you will hear and take notes on a two-part lecture by Edward Sullivan, a former elected official from the state of New York. The title of his lecture is *The Structure of the U.S. Federal Government*. First Mr. Sullivan will describe the three branches of the U.S. government. Then he will explain the system of checks and balances.

BEFORE THE LECTURE

⌒ LISTENING FOR THE PLAN OF A LECTURE

> Good lecturers usually begin by stating the main topics they plan to talk about. They often use phrases like these to signal their plan:
>
> *What I'm going to do today is . . .*
> *Today, I'm going to discuss . . .*
> *First, I'm going to . . .*
> *First, I plan to . . .*
> *Then, I'll talk about . . .*
> *After that . . .*
> *Next, we'll look at . . .*
> *Finally, I'll . . .*

1 Form complete sentences from the introduction to Edward Sullivan's lecture by matching each item on the left with the item on the right that completes it.

_____ **1** What I'm going to do today is

_____ **2** And that way, you can start to

_____ **3** First, I'll introduce the three

_____ **4** And I'll be using

_____ **5** And then, after that, I'll explain

a understand how it works.

b give you an overview of how the government is organized.

c branches of government.

d the system of checks and balances.

e this chart here on the board to help you understand.

2 Now listen to the introduction to the lecture and check your answers to step 1.
▶ PLAY

NOTE TAKING: USING INFORMATION THE LECTURER PUTS ON THE BOARD

Lecturers often write important information on the board, and you should include this information in your notes. As soon as you enter the classroom and sit down, take out your writing materials and copy anything the lecturer has written on the board into your notebook. As the lecture continues, copy anything else the lecturer writes on the board into your notes.

Before the lecture, Mr. Sullivan put a chart like the one below on the board. Copy the chart onto your own paper. You will use it to take notes when you listen to the first part of the lecture. (Notice that some of the information has already been filled in for you as an example.)

Branch of Government	Legislative	Executive	Judicial
Name	Congress: – Senate – House of Representatives		
Name of officials	Senators Representatives		
Responsibilities	makes laws		
Details	Senate = 100 members (2 from each state) House = 435 members (number depends on size of state population)		

LECTURE, PART ONE: The Three Branches of the U.S. Federal Government

GUESSING VOCABULARY FROM CONTEXT

When you listen to a lecture, there will usually be some words you do not understand. Sometimes, however, you can guess the meaning of an unfamiliar word by using your knowledge of related words or the context, that is, the phrases and sentences around the unknown word. When a speaker uses a word you do not know, listen carefully for the following "context clues":

- an example
- an explanation
- a definition
- an explanation
- a paraphrase (a restatement using different or easier words)

1 | The following items contain important vocabulary from Part One of the lecture. Work with a partner. Using the context and your knowledge of related words, take turns trying to guess the meanings of the words in **bold**.

_____ 1 I'm going to . . . give you an **overview** of how the federal government is organized.

_____ 2 **Obviously**, states with larger populations, like California, have more representatives.

_____ 3 The executive branch . . . "executes," or **approves** the laws that Congress makes.

_____ 4 **Besides** the President, the executive branch also includes the Vice President . . .

_____ 5 The executive branch also includes . . . the heads of government **departments**.

_____ 6 There are three levels of **courts** in the United States.

_____ 7 Their job is to **interpret** the laws passed by Congress . . .

_____ 8 . . . in other words, to decide if a law is **constitutional** or not.

2 | Work with your partner. Match the **bold** terms in the sentences in step 1 with their definitions below. If necessary, use a dictionary to check your answers.

    a clearly, of course
    b allows, accepts
    c follows, or agrees with, the Constitution of the United States
    d in addition to
    e part of the government that deals with one specific area
    f general description
    g the place where judges listen to legal cases
    h decide on the exact meaning of (a law)

🎧 NOTE TAKING: USING INFORMATION THE LECTURER PUTS ON THE BOARD

1 | Listen to Part One of the lecture. In the chart you copied into your notebook, fill in the missing information. (Note: There will not be information for all the boxes.)
▶ **PLAY**

2 | With your partner, review the information you wrote in your chart and use it to write six complete sentences about the lecture content.
Example:
The responsibility of the legislative branch is to make laws.

LECTURE, PART TWO: *The System of Checks and Balances*

GUESSING VOCABULARY FROM CONTEXT

1 | The following items contain important vocabulary from Part Two of the lecture. Work with a partner. Using the context and your knowledge of related words, take turns trying to guess the meanings of the words in **bold**.

_____ 1 The Founding Fathers . . . wanted to avoid a **dictatorship**.

_____ 2 Let's **suppose** Congress passes a law, but the President doesn't want to approve it.

_____ 3 Sometimes someone **challenges** the constitutionality of a law.

_____ 4 Most cases like that will be **heard** in a lower-level court.

_____ 5 The Supreme Court has the final **authority** to decide if the law . . . is either constitutional or unconstitutional.

2 | Work with your partner. Match the **bold** terms in the previous sentences with their definitions that follow. If necessary, use a dictionary to check your answers.

a rule by one party or person
b power
c judged
d imagine
e questions, does not want to accept

🎧 NOTE TAKING: TAKING GOOD LECTURE NOTES

Learning to take good notes takes time and practice. Everyone has a unique way of taking notes, but almost everyone follows these guidelines:

- Write only important words, not complete sentences.
- Be sure to include main ideas, examples, and important details.
- Use abbreviations and symbols.

One useful way to take notes is to indent examples and details.

1 | Look at a student's notes as you listen to Part Two of the lecture. ▶ **PLAY**

> ### The System of Checks and Balances
>
> Why is fed. gov. divided into branches?
> > Founders wanted to avoid dictatorship.
> > Invented system of checks & balances.
>
> Def. the 3 branches
> > have sep. respons. +
> > have power to check (limit) each other's actions
>
> Ex.:
> > 1. Selection of Supreme Court Justices
> > > –Pres. chooses Justices, but Cong. can disapprove
> > 2. Cong. passes laws, but Pres. can veto
> > 3. Cong. passes law & Pres. signs, but Supreme Court can say it's unconstitutional

2 | Work with a partner. Find places where the note-taker
- wrote only important words instead of complete sentences
- wrote main ideas
- used abbreviations and symbols
- indented examples and details

AFTER THE LECTURE

SHARING YOUR KNOWLEDGE

Work in small groups. Look at the pictures of the three branches of the U.S. government. Tell each other what you see and share what you have learned about each branch.

The U.S. Congress
(Legislative branch)

The President
(Executive branch)

The Supreme Court
(Judicial branch)

Chapter **2**

Constitutional Issues Today

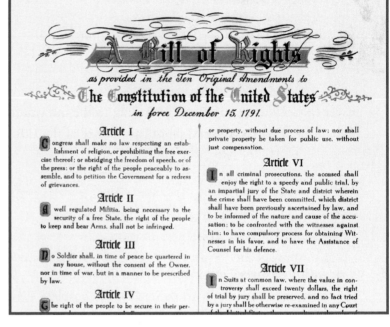

1 GETTING STARTED

In this section, you are going to read background information about the U.S. Constitution and listen to a time line about some important events in U.S. constitutional history.

READING AND THINKING ABOUT THE TOPIC

1 | Read the following passage.

In 1776, the 13 American colonies declared their independence from Britain. This act led to the Revolutionary War (1775–1783), which the British lost. In 1786, George Washington, James Madison, Alexander Hamilton, and other leaders of the time met in Philadelphia to discuss how to organize the government of the new country, the United States of America. Their work produced the document that set up the structure of government in the United States: the U.S. Constitution. The writers knew that changes to the Constitution would be necessary from time to time as the country grew and changed. Therefore, they created a process for changing, or amending, the original document. Twenty-six amendments have been added since the Constitution was signed. The first 10 amendments, added in 1791, are called the *Bill of Rights*. Freedom of speech, freedom of religion, and the right of people accused of crimes to have a lawyer are just three of the basic rights guaranteed by these amendments.

Some parts of the Bill of Rights are controversial today. That is, Americans do not always agree about the correct way to interpret them. For example, according to the

Fourth Amendment, government officials, such as police officers, cannot enter people's homes or listen to their phone conversations without permission from a judge. However, some Americans believe the government should be able to do these things if it is looking for information that can help stop terrorism.

Censorship, or limiting freedom of expression in speech, writing, or art, is another example of a controversial issue. For example, some cities and states have tried to pass laws allowing the censorship of works of art or literature that the citizens of those places thought were offensive. Yet these laws conflict with the First Amendment, which gives Americans freedom of speech and freedom of the press.

Whenever there are conflicts like these, it is the responsibility of the courts to decide what is constitutional and what is not.

2 Answer the following questions according to the information in the passage:
  1 What does the passage say about the history of the U.S. Constitution?
  2 What is the Bill of Rights?
  3 What are some controversial topics in the U.S. Constitution?

3 Read these questions and share your answers with a partner:
  1 Do you think it is important for a country to have a written constitution?
  2 Do you know of any countries that have a constitution similar to the constitution of the United States?

⌒ UNDERSTANDING NUMBERS, DATES, AND TIME EXPRESSIONS

Numbers that are used for counting are called cardinal numbers. Numbers that are used for describing an order are called ordinal numbers. Numbers can be hard to understand in rapid speech, so it is useful to review their pronunciation.

Cardinal numbers	**Ordinal numbers**
"1" is said as *one.*	*first (twenty-first, thirty-first, etc.)*
"2" is said as *two.*	*second (twenty-second, thirty-second, etc.)*
"3" is said as *three.*	*third (twenty-third, thirty-third, etc.)*
"4" is said as *four.*	*fourth (fifth, sixth, seventh, etc.; twenty-fourth, twenty-fifth, etc.)*

Dates

"1876" is said as *eighteen seventy-six.*

"2004" is said as *two thousand four.*

"July 4, 1776" is said as *July fourth, seventeen seventy-six.*

Time expressions

in is used with years	*in 1776*
on is used with dates	*on July 4*
during is used with a period of time	*during the 1960s*
between . . . and . . .	*between 1960 and 1990*
from . . . to . . .	*from 1960 to 1990*

1 The following time line shows some important events in U.S. constitutional history. Work in small groups and see if you know or can guess any of the dates. If you think you know a date, fill it in.

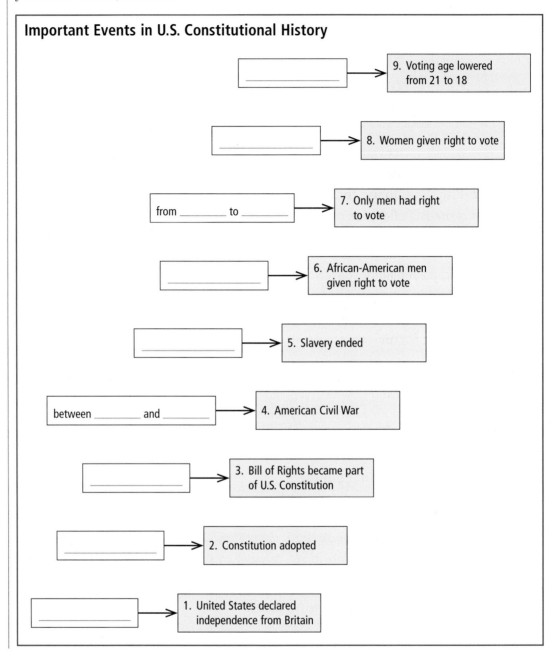

Important Events in U.S. Constitutional History

9. Voting age lowered from 21 to 18

8. Women given right to vote

from _____ to _____

7. Only men had right to vote

6. African-American men given right to vote

5. Slavery ended

between _____ and _____

4. American Civil War

3. Bill of Rights became part of U.S. Constitution

2. Constitution adopted

1. United States declared independence from Britain

2 Listen to the time line. Write the dates you hear. ▶ **PLAY**

3 Work with a partner. Practice repeating the information in the time line. Focus on the correct way of saying numbers, dates, and time expressions.

Example:
On July 4, 1776, the United States declared its independence from Britain.

2 AMERICAN VOICES: Magda, Hang, and Gloria

In this section, you will hear three people – Magda, Hang, and Gloria – talk about constitutional rights that are important to them.

BEFORE THE INTERVIEWS

PREVIEWING THE TOPIC

1 Read the following list. It shows some legal rights that Americans have. If you are American, you can

_____ **a** send a letter criticizing the President to a newspaper.

_____ **b** speak to a lawyer if you are arrested by the police.

_____ **c** buy a gun to use for sport or self-protection.

_____ **d** refuse to allow the police to enter your home without permission from a judge.

_____ **e** listen to music with violent or sexual words.

_____ **f** hang a religious symbol outside your house.

_____ **g** wear any clothes you choose.

_____ **h** refuse to answer questions that a judge asks you in court.

_____ **i** look at pictures on the Internet of people in intimate situations.

2 Read the information below about some of the amendments in the Bill of Rights. Fill in the blanks in step 1 with the number of the amendment that gives Americans each right.

First Amendment	People have freedom of religion, speech, and the press.
Second Amendment	People have the right to "bear arms," that is, to own guns.
Fourth Amendment	People have the right to "be secure in their persons, houses, papers, and effects." This means citizens have the right to privacy and safety in their homes.
Fifth Amendment	In court, a person accused of a crime cannot be forced to speak against himself or herself.
Sixth Amendment	People accused of a crime have the right to a speedy (fast) and public trial by jury, and they have the right to be defended by a lawyer.

3 Work in small groups and compare your answers. Then discuss the following questions:

1 Do you think the rights listed above are important? Why or why not?

2 Are there countries you know about where people don't have these rights? Explain.

INTERVIEW WITH MAGDA AND HANG: Important constitutional rights

Magda

Hang

Here are some words and phrases from the interview printed in **bold** and given in the context in which you will hear them. They are followed by definitions.

I believe **censorship** is wrong . . . I don't think anyone has the right to tell people what they can see: *prohibiting or limiting the free expression of words or ideas*

Art is a powerful way of expressing ideas, and ideas can **be very controversial**: *create a lot of disagreement*

The government has always censored **violent** photographs during wartime: *using force to hurt or attack*

There was an **exhibit** called "Sensation" in a museum in New York: *art show*

There were paintings and **sculptures** . . . that were very **offensive** to some people: *works of art made out of stone, metal, wood, etc. / unpleasant, insulting*

The **mayor** tried to close the exhibit: *the elected leader of a town or city*

I value the fact that in the United States we have **freedom of assembly**: *the freedom to meet in groups*

This includes the right to **demonstrate** and **complain** and demand change: *express strong opinions about issues in public, especially by marching in the streets in large groups / say you are unhappy or dissatisfied*

The students wanted the university to stop buying products from companies that use **child labor**: *child workers, for example in factories*

The university changed its **policy**: *rules, official way of doing something*

So you see, our **protests** were very effective: *demonstrations, complaints*

🎧 LISTENING FOR SPECIFIC INFORMATION

Sometimes textbooks or teachers provide lists of questions to help you focus on specific information in a listening passage or lecture. Read the questions before listening so that you know what information to listen for. Then use your background knowledge to try to predict the correct answers. These strategies can help you become a more efficient listener.

1 Read the following incomplete sentences and the two possible ways to complete them.

1 The constitutional right that Magda mentions is _____.
   a the right to attend public protests
   b the right to freedom of speech

2 Magda is a _____.
   a photographer
   b painter

3 Magda thinks that _____.
   a artists should be able to paint or draw anything they like
   b it's necessary to censor some types of art

4 Magda says that censorship _____.
   a happens all the time
   b is not very common

5 Hang says that U.S. citizens have _____.
   a freedom of assembly
   b the right to practice any religion they choose

6 Recently, students at Hang's university _____.
   a protested the university's policies
   b wrote a letter to the college president

7 Hang is concerned about child labor _____.
   a in the United States
   b in other countries

2 Now listen to the interview. Listen for the answers that correctly complete the sentences and circle them. Then work with a partner and check your answers.
   ▶ PLAY

3 Discuss these questions in small groups: Do you agree with Magda and Hang's opinions? Why or why not?

INTERVIEW WITH GLORIA: Another important right

Gloria

> Here are some words and phrases from the interview printed in **bold** and given in the context in which you will hear them. They are followed by definitions.
>
> Can you **identify** an important constitutional right?: *name*
>
> . . . the right to **bear arms**: *have a gun*
>
> One [group] is **criminals**: *people who act against the law*
>
> Some people have guns for sports, like **hunting** or **target shooting**: *chasing and killing animals for food or sport / shooting a gun at an object for sport*

🎧 LISTENING FOR SPECIFIC INFORMATION

1 Before you listen to the interview with Gloria, read the paragraph below and predict the kind of information you need to listen for.

> Gloria focuses on the right to (1) _____. She believes the (2) _____ Amendment gives American citizens this right. Gloria says there are (3) _____ groups of people who own guns. One group is (4) _____, and they will own guns whether it is (5) _____ or not. The second group is (6) _____ people who own guns for (7) _____ reasons, for example, for (8) _____ or for (9) _____. Gloria explains that the (10) _____ can't be everywhere, so some people might feel that they (11) _____ a gun to protect themselves.

2 Listen to the interview. Fill in the blanks with the missing words or expressions. Then work with a partner and check your responses. ▶ PLAY

3 Discuss Gloria's opinion in small groups. Do you agree or disagree with her? Why?

AFTER THE INTERVIEWS

UNDERSTANDING HUMOR ABOUT THE TOPIC

If you can understand and appreciate humor, such as cartoons or jokes, about a topic, it means that you have probably understood the main points of the topic.

1 | Look at the cartoon and read the caption.

"The way I see it, the Constitution cuts both ways. The First Amendment gives you the right to say what you want, but the Second Amendment gives me the right to shoot you for it."

2 | Work with a partner or a small group and answer the following questions:
  1 Where are the people in the cartoon? What are they doing?
  2 What does the speaker mean when he says the Constitution "cuts both ways"?
  3 Is the speaker's description of the First and Second Amendments correct?
  4 Is the speaker serious? How do you know?
  5 Do you think the cartoon is funny? Why or why not?

3 IN YOUR OWN VOICE

In this section, you will participate in role plays about two controversial situations. Then you will share your opinions about the situations with your classmates.

ROLE PLAYING

Role playing is a conversation activity in which you pretend that you are a person in an imaginary situation, for example, an angry customer complaining about a mistake in your telephone bill. Role playing gives you an opportunity to practice new vocabulary and develop your communication skills. This will give you confidence when you need to use the same language and skills in the real world.

1 | Read the situations below.

> SITUATION 1: A MEETING AT SCHOOL
> "A" is a student at a public high school who is very critical of the government's policies. The student wears a shirt making a joke about the President to school. Another student, "B," is offended by the joke on the shirt and tells his or her parents about it. Then B's parents call the school and complain to the principal. The principal invites all four parents to a meeting to discuss the issue. The principal must decide whether to ask A to stop wearing the shirt to school.
>
> Roles:
> - Student A's parents, who believe the student has the constitutional right to wear the shirt
> - Student B's parents, who are offended by student A's shirt
> - The principal, who listens to both sides and must make a decision

> SITUATION 2: A CONVERSATION BETWEEN PARENTS
> "A," a 10-year-old, often goes to play at the home of "B," a neighbor. One day A's parents discover that B's parents own a gun. B's parents say the gun is locked in a cabinet, but A's parents are worried about allowing their child to play at the neighbor's house. They decide to talk to B's parents because they must decide whether to allow their child to play at B's house.
>
> Roles:
> - A's parents, who ask B's parents to remove the gun from their home.
> - B's parents, who feel they need the gun for protection.

2 | Work in small groups. Select one of the situations to role-play. Decide who will play each role. Practice your role play in your group.

3 | Perform your role play for another group or the class.

4 | Discuss the situations with members of your class. What would you want if you were the parents in these situations?

4 ACADEMIC LISTENING AND NOTE TAKING: The First Amendment

In this section, you will hear and take notes on a two-part lecture by Marcella Bencivenni, a professor of U.S. history. The title of her lecture is *The First Amendment*. Professor Bencivenni will give an overview of the First Amendment to the Constitution and discuss some controversies that surround it.

BEFORE THE LECTURE

PREDICTING WHAT YOU WILL HEAR

Thinking about the topic and trying to predict what you will hear will greatly increase your understanding.

1 Read the following excerpts from introductions to newspaper articles based on true stories.

1
Protest for Immigrant Rights
Last Friday, the streets of Los Angeles were filled with hundreds of thousands of people protesting the government's policies on immigration. . . .

4
Newspaper Publishes Controversial Cartoon
Although a recent cartoon was likely to offend some religious groups, a newspaper made the decision to publish it. . . .

2
Cell Phones in Classrooms? Yes, Say Parents
Although many principals want students to leave their cell phones at home, parents disagree. They say they need to be able to contact their children in an emergency. . . .

5
Police Officer Fired for Wearing Religious Symbol on Uniform
After receiving two warnings, a Texas police officer was fired for wearing a small religious symbol on the collar of his police uniform. . . .

3
Library Moves Book to Top Shelf
To Kill a Mockingbird, Harper Lee's classic American novel about discrimination and personal choice, has too much sex and disturbing racial themes, according to some readers. . . .

2 With a partner, discuss the following questions:
   1 In each article, what rights are exercised by the people involved?
   2 Do you think any of these topics is controversial? Why or why not?
   3 Based on these excerpts, what topics do you think the lecturer will discuss?

⋒ NOTE TAKING: LISTENING FOR MAIN IDEAS AND SUPPORTING DETAILS

Remember that **main ideas** are the important points a speaker wants to make. A lecturer may present a main idea as a statement or as a question. Supporting details explain, describe, or prove main ideas. Supporting details often consist of examples, reasons, explanations, and stories. For example:

Main idea (statement):
I'm going to talk about a very important right: freedom of speech.
    Supporting detail (reason / explanation):
    Freedom of speech is protected by the Bill of Rights.

Main idea (question):
What does freedom of speech mean?
    Supporting detail (example):
    We are all free to express our ideas even if other people strongly disagree.

1 | Below are two excerpts from the lecture. The sentences are not in the correct order. Read the sentences and write the number 1 next to the main idea. Then predict the order of the other sentences by writing the numbers 2–6 in the blanks.

Excerpt 1

_____ For instance, an employer can't hire you or fire you just because he likes or doesn't like your religion.
_____ What does it mean to have freedom of religion?
_____ What I mean is that Americans are free to wear any kind of religious clothing they prefer.
_____ Now this freedom affects Americans in many ways.
_____ Basically it means two things: First, Americans are free to practice their religion without interference from the government, and second, there is no national religion.
_____ And freedom of religion even includes how you dress.

Excerpt 2

_____ In fact, the courts have said that freedom of speech includes all forms of expression, meaning words, pictures, music, even the way you wear your hair!
_____ You're also free to read or listen to other people's ideas.
_____ The next freedom listed in the First Amendment is maybe the most famous one, because it's the one that all of us practice every single day, and that's freedom of speech.
_____ But in addition, freedom of speech includes what we call "symbolic" speech – like wearing the clothes you like.
_____ Basically, it means you are free to talk openly about your ideas, even if other people disagree with them.
_____ What does that mean, exactly?

2 Listen to the two excerpts. Check to see if you correctly selected the main idea and if you placed the other sentences in the correct order. ▶ **PLAY**

LECTURE, PART ONE: Overview of the First Amendment

GUESSING VOCABULARY FROM CONTEXT

1 The following items contain important vocabulary from Part One of the lecture. Work with a partner. Using the context and your knowledge of related words, take turns trying to guess the meanings of the words in **bold**.

_____ **1** The First Amendment **affects** the way we live every day.

_____ **2** I'll tell you about some **cases** that will show you why the First Amendment is so controversial.

_____ **3** The First Amendment **guarantees** . . . five basic freedoms.

_____ **4** Americans are free to practice their religion without **interference** from the government.

_____ **5** An employer can't **hire** or fire you . . . because [of] your religion.

_____ **6** Both of these forms of **expression** are legal.

_____ **7** Freedom of **the press** means . . . to freely publish different ideas and opinions.

_____ **8** It's . . . legal for a **journalist** to write an article criticizing the government.

_____ **9** You can open the newspaper any day and find articles that **criticize** the government.

_____ **10** You can [read an article about American] **military** activities in other countries.

2 Work with a partner. Match the vocabulary terms with their definitions by writing the letter of each definition below in the blank next to the sentence containing the correct term in step 1. Check your answers in a dictionary if necessary.

    a a writer for a magazine or newspaper
    b influences, has an effect on
    c unwanted involvement or participation
    d give someone a job
    e say negative things about someone or something
    f promises
    g relating to soldiers or war
    h written materials that bring people news; also, the people who write these materials
    i situations, examples
    j communication of thoughts or feelings

🎧 NOTE TAKING: USING SYMBOLS AND ABBREVIATIONS

When you are taking notes during a lecture, you have to write down a lot of information very quickly. To save time, use symbols and abbreviations whenever you can. Some forms are commonly used. Here are some examples:

Common symbols

+ *or* &	and	. . .	and so on, etc.
%	percent	→	leads to, causes
∴	therefore	"	ditto (same as above)
=	equals, is, has	↑, ↓	increase, decrease
≠	not, not the same as	>, <	more than, less than

Common abbreviations

e.g., *or* ex:	for example	w/	with
b/c	because	w/o	without
esp.	especially	etc.	and so on
imp.	important	i.e.,	that is (in other words)
vs	versus (against)	yr.	year
pt	part	inc.	include, including
sum	summary, summarize		

1 Study the following list of important words and suggested abbreviations from Part One of the lecture.

Word	Abbreviation	Word	Abbreviation	Word	Abbreviation
amendment	amend	freedom	f'dom	religion	relig
different	diff	students	sts	president	pres
government	gov't	Americans	Ams	expression	exp
speech	spch	representatives	reps	group	grp
includes, including	inc.				

2 Read the incomplete notes on the next page. Work in pairs and predict which symbols or abbreviations from the box and step 1 will go in the blanks.

3 Listen to Part One of the lecture. Complete the notes, using symbols and abbreviations from the box and step 1. ▶ PLAY

4 Work with a partner and compare your answers. Summarize the First Amendment in your own words.

1st _____ = 5 f'doms

1. F'dom of _____
   = _____ can practice their _____ _____
   interference from _____
   U.S. has no national _____

2. F'dom of _____
   = _____ to talk openly about ideas
   Inc. "symbolic speech" — _____ clothes
   _____ all forms of _____ , e.g., words, pictures, etc.

3. _____ of the press
   = _____ to publish _____ ideas & opinions
   Inc. books, newspaper, magazines, Internet
   _____ , cartoon making joke about _____
   journalist can write article criticizing the _____

4. _____ of assembly
   = can meet in _____
   _____ , college _____ demonstrate

5. _____ of petition
   = citizens have _____ to ask _____ to change things

To sum: we use the term _____ of _____ to talk about all
5 f'doms.

LECTURE, PART TWO: First Amendment Controversies

GUESSING VOCABULARY FROM CONTEXT

1 │ The following items contain important vocabulary from Part Two of the lecture.
Work with a partner. Using the context and your knowledge of related words, take
turns trying to guess the meanings of the words in **bold**.

_____ 1 **In practice**, there are some restrictions [on freedom of speech].

_____ 2 They think flag burning is **unpatriotic** and insults the government.

_____ 3 The Supreme Court has **ruled** that flag burning is legal.

_____ 4 Many teachers and principals . . . have tried to **forbid** cell phones
[at school].

_____ 5 Parents . . . need to have a way to **get in touch with** their children.

_____ 6 [Should] children have the right to say prayers in **public schools**?

2 Work with your partner. Match the vocabulary terms with their definitions by writing the letter of each definition below in the blank next to the sentence containing the correct term in step 1. Check your answers in a dictionary if necessary.

    a not allow
    b contact (for example, by phone)
    c in reality; the way people actually do something
    d acting or speaking against the government
    e decided (a legal case)
    f free or inexpensive schools that are paid for by taxes

⌒ NOTE TAKING: USING A MAP TO ORGANIZE YOUR NOTES

> Some people like to take notes using a method called *mapping*. One way to make a map is to write the topic or the main idea in the center of the page. The supporting details are written under, over, or next to the main idea. Related ideas are connected by lines.

1 Below is a section of a student's map for Part Two of the lecture. Study the map with a partner and answer these questions: What is this part of the lecture about? How many examples are given? What is the meaning of *no* and *yes*? What information is missing?

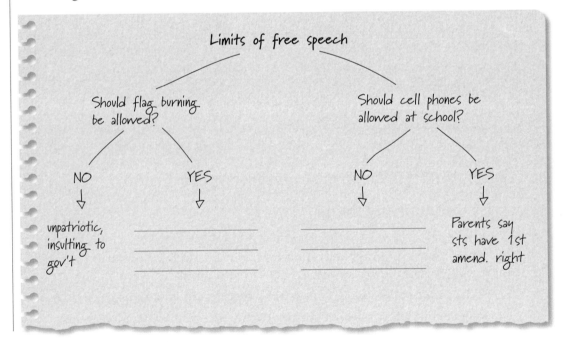

2 Now look at another section of the map. Answer these questions with your partner: What is the main idea? What is the example? Where do you predict you will need to draw lines to connect ideas?

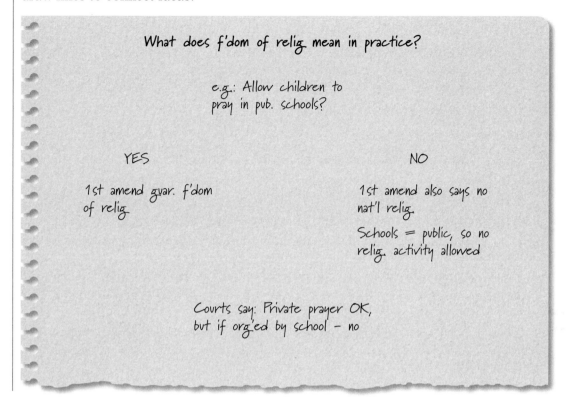

3 Listen to Part Two of the lecture. Fill in the missing information in step 1. Draw in the missing lines in step 2. ▶ PLAY

4 Work in small groups and compare answers. Then use the maps to answer these questions:

1 What are the limits of free speech?

2 What does freedom of religion mean in practice?

AFTER THE LECTURE

CONDUCTING A SURVEY

The purpose of a survey is to collect information in order to compare the opinions of different individuals or groups of people. Surveys usually consist of questions for interviewees to answer or statements that interviewees are asked to agree or disagree with. Interviewers often ask follow-up questions to allow the interviewees to give more information or explain their opinions.

1 You are going to survey three people outside your class about four controversial questions:

   1 Do you think it should be legal to burn the flag as a form of political protest?

   2 Do you think children should be allowed to bring cell phones to school?

   3 Do you think teachers and students in public schools should have the right to say a prayer together at the beginning of the school day?

   4 Do you think the government should be allowed to listen to people's telephone conversations?

2 On your own paper, make four charts like the one below, one for each question.

Question:		
Person	**Opinion**	**Reason**
	YES NOT SURE NO	
	YES NOT SURE NO	
	YES NOT SURE NO	

3 Try to talk to people of different ages and backgrounds. Here is a way to start:

Hi. I'm doing a survey for my English class about controversial issues. May I ask you a few questions? Please answer yes, no, *or* I'm not sure.

4 After a person has answered a question, follow up by asking "Why?" Take notes on the person's reason(s) in your chart.

5 Explain the results of your survey to a small group or to the class. Give your own opinion about the questions as well.

A Diverse Nation

Unit 2

The Statue of Liberty in New York Harbor

American society is composed of people from many cultural and ethnic groups. In this unit, you will learn about some of these groups. Chapter 3 concerns the wave of immigration to the United States that lasted from the mid-nineteenth to the early twentieth century. You will hear interviews with Americans whose families left Europe during that time to begin new lives in this country. The lecture is about the prejudice those immigrants faced and the contributions they made to American life and culture. In Chapter 4, you will hear the voices of Americans who arrived in the next wave of immigration, which began during the second half of the twentieth century and continues today. The lecture is about how these new immigrants have become part of American society while keeping their connections to their countries and cultures of origin.

3

The Origins of Diversity

Lewis W. Hine was famous for his photography of the immigrant experience during the early part of the twentieth century.

Lewis W. Hine 1874-1940

1 GETTING STARTED

In this section, you are going to read some background information about late nineteenth and early twentieth century immigration to the United States. You will also hear numerical information and examine graphs about this wave of immigration.

READING AND THINKING ABOUT THE TOPIC

1 | Read the following passage.

> The United States is a country of immigrants. Its people come from a variety of religious, economic, racial, and ethnic backgrounds.
>
> In the late fifteenth century, British and European immigrants began to come to America. These immigrants, or settlers, brought hundreds of thousands of people from Africa to work as slaves. When the settlers arrived, they encountered various tribes of Native Americans. Many Native Americans died either from diseases brought by the settlers or because of wars with the settlers over land.
>
> From the 1840s to the 1920s, another big wave of immigration occurred. This wave of immigrants included Germans, Irish, Italians, and Jews. Smaller groups of Chinese and Mexican immigrants also came to America. Some came in search of better economic opportunities, while others came for political or religious freedom. Some groups were welcomed, and others were rejected. However, they all left their mark on America's economy, society, and culture.

2 Answer the following questions according to the information in the passage:

1 Why is the United States considered a country of immigrants?

2 What were the largest groups of immigrants to come to the United States between the 1840s and the 1920s? Why did they come?

3 Read these questions and share your answers with a partner:

1 Do you know of anyone who immigrated to America in the late nineteenth or early twentieth centuries ? Why did they come? What were their experiences?

2 What do you think would be the most difficult thing about leaving your country and going somewhere else to live?

BUILDING BACKGROUND KNOWLEDGE

Work with a partner and read the list of factors that affected immigration to the United States from 1840 to 1930. Do you think these events led to an increase or decrease in immigration? Write ↑ (increase) or ↓ (decrease) in the blank next to each factor.

_____ There was not enough food in parts of Europe in the 1840s.

_____ Beginning in the 1880s, steamships made it faster and easier to cross the Atlantic Ocean.

_____ During the 1880s, there was violence against Jews in Russia.

_____ World War I began in Europe in 1914.

_____ The United States entered the war in 1917.

_____ In the 1920s, there were important changes in U.S. laws that limited immigration.

_____ In 1929, the American stock market "crashed." This was the beginning of the effects of the Great Depression in the United States. Millions of Americans lost their money and their jobs, and it was almost impossible to find work.

🎧 LISTENING FOR NUMERICAL INFORMATION

Listening for numbers and dates can be very difficult in a second language. Here are some suggestions to help you to understand numerical information about history.

1 Learn the words and phrases often used to refer to time periods:

century = 100 years   *decade* = 10 years

twentieth century = 1900–1999   *figure* = number

the mid-1930s = around 1935   *the early 1940s* = 1940–1943

2 Learn verbs that often describe numbers:

go up = increase, rise, climb

go down = decrease, fall, decline

1 Work with a partner and look at the three graphs below. One of them shows the correct pattern of immigration to the United States from 1820 to 2000, according to the U.S. Bureau of the Census. The other two are incorrect. Use your background knowledge to help you guess which graph shows the correct pattern.

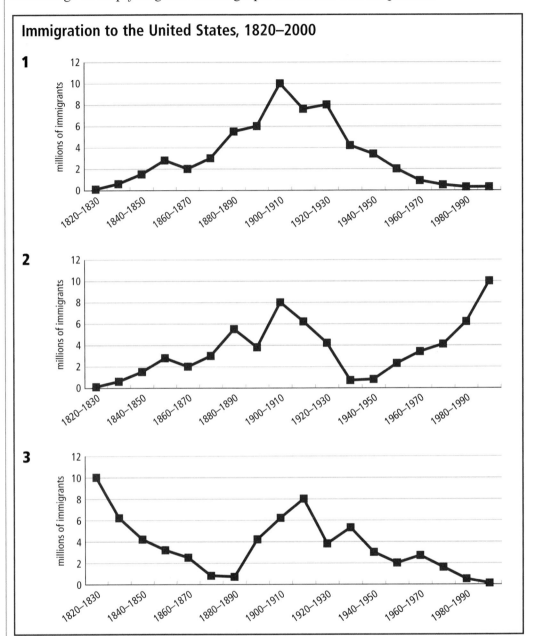

Immigration to the United States, 1820–2000

2 Listen to a description of immigration patterns to the United States. Circle the number of the one graph that matches the information you hear. ▶ PLAY

3 Work with a partner and compare answers. Then discuss this question: What is the main difference between immigration patterns to the United States in the nineteenth and the twentieth centuries?

AMERICAN VOICES: Patrick, Eunice, and John

In this section, you will hear three Americans of different ethnic and cultural backgrounds discuss the experiences of their families, who settled in the United States in the late nineteenth and early twentieth centuries.

BEFORE THE INTERVIEWS

BUILDING BACKGROUND KNOWLEDGE

1 Read these two sets of factors that influence immigration:

"Push" factors: reasons people leave their home countries

    a economic   **b** political   **c** religious   **d** other

"Pull" factors: reasons people want to come to the United States

    a economic   **b** political   **c** religious   **d** other

2 Work with a partner and read the statements below. Match each statement with one of the factors in step 1 by putting the correct letter in the appropriate column.

Push	Pull		
	a	1	My great-grandparents came from Italy around 1890. There were more jobs in the United States.
		2	Many people in my grandparents' village in Russia were attacked because of their religious beliefs.
		3	My mother came over to the States to meet up with my father. They were in love and planned to get married.
		4	My parents came from a farming village in Greece because there wasn't enough land there for people to farm.
		5	In 1848, there was a potato famine in Ireland. All the potato plants died, and there was very little food for years after that.
		6	The United States is a democracy. We could vote for whoever we wanted to.
		7	In the village we came from, it was dangerous to express your real opinions.

EXAMINING GRAPHIC MATERIAL

1 Look at the two pie charts on the next page. They show where immigrants to the United States came from during two important periods: from 1840 to 1860 and from 1880 to 1900.

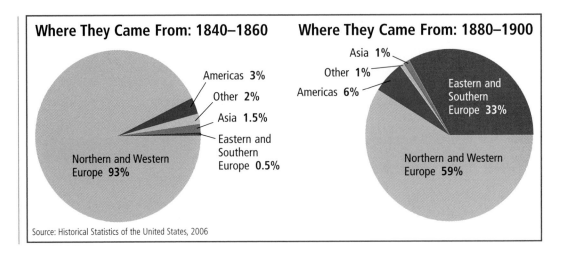

Where They Came From: 1840–1860

- Americas **3%**
- Other **2%**
- Asia **1.5%**
- Eastern and Southern Europe **0.5%**
- Northern and Western Europe **93%**

Where They Came From: 1880–1900

- Asia **1%**
- Other **1%**
- Americas **6%**
- Eastern and Southern Europe **33%**
- Northern and Western Europe **59%**

Source: Historical Statistics of the United States, 2006

2 Underline or circle the choice that correctly completes the statements. Then work with a partner and compare your answers.

1 From 1840 to 1860, most immigrants came from [northern and western Europe / the Americas / Asia / eastern and southern Europe / other places].

2 Most immigrants from eastern and southern Europe came to the United States in the period [1840–1860 / 1880–1900].

3 From 1840 to 1900, the percentage of immigrants from the Americas [rose a little / stayed exactly the same / fell quickly].

4 The percentage of immigrants from Asia [increased a lot / stayed about the same / fell sharply] during the 1840–1900 time period.

INTERVIEW WITH PATRICK: Immigration to the United States in the 1860s

Here are some words and phrases from the interview with Patrick printed in **bold** and given in the context in which you will hear them. They are followed by definitions.

There had been a potato **famine** [in Ireland]: *a time when there is not enough food, and people die as a result*

There was just no food, and people were **desperate**: *without hope*

About a million people died – **can you imagine**?: *can you believe that?*

So the Irish started coming over in **massive** numbers: *very large*

They **stuck together**: *they helped each other*

They depended on each other to **survive**: *live*

They were Catholic. That **set them apart**: *made them different from the rest of the people*

I've heard there was a lot of **prejudice** against them: *negative feelings or opinions*

On the other hand, they **made a lot of contributions to society**: *worked hard to help their families and society*

⌂ ANSWERING TRUE/FALSE QUESTIONS

True/false questions can be confusing, so be sure to read them carefully before answering. Remember these guidelines:

- If part of the statement is false, then the entire statement is false.
- Absolute statements (statements that use words like *all, always, never, nobody*) are usually false.

1 | Read the statements below before you listen to the interview with Patrick.

_____ **1** Patrick's grandparents met in the United States.

_____ **2** Patrick's family came to the United States for political reasons.

_____ **3** Some of Patrick's relatives stayed in Ireland after his grandparents immigrated to the United States.

_____ **4** The potato famine happened before Patrick's grandparents left Ireland.

_____ **5** Many immigrants arrived with less than $50.

_____ **6** Most Irish immigrants were Catholic.

_____ **7** Irish immigrants all worked as farmers.

_____ **8** Patrick comes from a small family.

Patrick

2 | Now listen to the interview. Mark each sentence *T* (true) or *F* (false). After listening, work with a partner. Compare answers and correct the false statements. ▶ **PLAY**

INTERVIEW WITH EUNICE AND JOHN: Immigration to the United States in the 1900s

Here are some words and phrases from the interview with Eunice and John printed in **bold** and given in the context in which you will hear them. They are followed by definitions.

There was always a fear of **religious persecution**: *being attacked because of your religious beliefs*

You'd **end up in jail**: *be sent to prison*

The economy was bad, and they couldn't **make a living**: *earn enough money to live*

The trip alone was a **nightmare**: *very difficult experience*

When they finally arrived, **they were almost penniless**: *they had very little money*

My grandmother . . . was **a midwife**: *a woman who helps other women when they are having a baby*

My father was a good student, and he ended up getting a **scholarship** to college: *a grant or gift of money to pay for college expenses*

As I **look back on it**, I see that . . . : *remember, think about something in the past*

My family **struggled hard**: *had to work very hard*

Eunice

John

🎧 LISTENING FOR SPECIFIC INFORMATION

1 | Look at the chart below before you listen to the interview with Eunice and John.

	Eunice	**John**
Ethnic or religious background	Jewish	
Country their relatives came from		
Reasons their relatives came to the United States		
Experience of their relatives in America		

2 | Now listen to the interview. Take notes in the chart based on what the speakers say. Then work with a partner and compare answers. **▶ PLAY**

AFTER THE INTERVIEWS

RETELLING WHAT YOU HAVE HEARD

1 | Review the tasks from the interviews with Patrick, Eunice, and John. In the space below, write one question that you would like to ask each speaker. You will use these questions in step 3.

Question for Patrick: _____

Question for Eunice: _____

Question for John: _____

2 | Form groups of three. Each member of the group should pretend to be one of the speakers from the interviews. When it is your turn to speak, explain:
- when and why your family immigrated to America
- what happened to your family after arriving in America

3 | Listen as your classmates ask you the questions they wrote. Answer the questions the way you imagine Patrick, Eunice, and John would answer them.

3 IN YOUR OWN VOICE

In this section, you will learn more about the experiences of the millions of immigrants who came to America during the late nineteenth and early twentieth centuries. First you will do some research about immigration during this period. Then you will pretend to be an immigrant and tell that person's story.

CONDUCTING RESEARCH

In academic classes, you will often be asked to do assignments or projects that involve research. You can use a library or the Internet to find information. When you find something useful, make sure you copy it accurately and always remember to write down the source of the information, that is, the book, magazine, newspaper, or Web site where you found the information.

1 | You are going to do research on Ellis Island, which is in New York City's harbor. Ellis Island was once the port of entry for millions of immigrants to the United States. Today it is a museum dedicated to telling the story of these immigrants.

2 | Work in four groups. Each group will be responsible for answering one of the following questions:

  a When did immigrants come through Ellis Island?

  b Which immigrant groups came through Ellis Island?

  c When and why did they come?

  d What happened to them when they arrived in the United States?

3 | Go to the Ellis Island Web site at www.ellisisland.org. Click on "Ellis Island" in the menu of options at the top of the page. From the pulldown menu, click on "Ellis Island History." If you do not have Internet access, read about Ellis Island in a library. Ask your librarian for help if necessary. Read and take notes on the answer to your assigned question.

4 | In class, form new groups of four consisting of one person who researched each of the four questions. Share the information you found with the other members of your group.

The main building at Ellis Island about 1900

Today the main building is an immigration museum.

APPLYING WHAT YOU HAVE LEARNED

Finding ways to apply what you have learned is a good way to deepen your understanding of a topic.

1 Look at the descriptions in the chart below of immigrants who came to America in the late nineteenth and early twentieth centuries. Select one of the immigrants and make up an imaginary story about his or her immigration experience based on the information provided. Make notes about your story. You can use these questions as a guide in making up your story:

- Was there one specific event that made you decide to leave your country?
- Was it difficult for you to leave?
- What are your hopes and dreams about your new life in America?
- What worries do you have about the future?

	Martin O'Reilly	**Salvatore Leo**	**Katya Prinz**	**Maria Karas**
Origin	Ireland	Italy	Poland	Greece
Age	25	17	60	10
Profession	carpenter	unemployed but is interested in engineering	seamstress	student
Family status	married	single	widow	single
Religion	Catholic	Catholic	Jewish	Greek Orthodox
Reason for coming	to escape the potato famine and start a new life	to avoid the army and go to a university	to join her son, who came three years earlier; and to enjoy religious freedom	to join other relatives from the same small village, where there were no jobs

Notes:

2 Work in groups. Tell your story to your classmates and listen to their stories.

4 ACADEMIC LISTENING AND NOTE TAKING: Immigrants to America Face Prejudice but Make Lasting Contributions

In this section, you will hear and take notes on a two-part lecture by Gerald Meyer, a professor of U.S. history. The title of his lecture is *Immigrants to America Face Prejudice but Make Lasting Contributions*. Professor Meyer will describe some of the experiences of late nineteenth- and early twentieth-century immigrants to the United States.

BEFORE THE LECTURE

BUILDING BACKGROUND KNOWLEDGE AND VOCABULARY

1 Below, on the left, is a handout showing a list of readings for Professor Meyer's history class on early immigration to the United States. Fill in the blanks with the missing unit titles and readings from the list on the right.

<table>
<tr>
<td>

**Early Immigration
to the United States**

Prof. G. Meyer

Assigned Readings

UNIT 1: _____

Readings:

1 <u>Strong Anti-Irish Sentiment Begins to Grow</u>

2 _____

3 _____

UNIT 2: _____

Readings:

1 <u>Many Unskilled Workers Needed for Nation's Infrastructure</u>

2 _____

3 _____

</td>
<td>

Unit Titles:
- Contributions of Immigrant Groups
- Prejudice Toward Immigrant Groups

Readings:
- Strong Anti-Irish Sentiment Begins to Grow
- Many Unskilled Workers Needed for Nation's Infrastructure
- Jobs in Construction and Services
- Needs of Agricultural and Industrial Production
- Widespread Anti-Immigrant Feelings
- Religious Prejudice and Stereotypes

</td>
</tr>
</table>

2 Work with a partner and compare answers. Use the information in the handout to predict what you will hear in the lecture.

◉ NOTE TAKING: LISTENING FOR TRANSITIONAL PHRASES THAT INTRODUCE SUPPORTING DETAILS

Supporting details consist of specific information such as reasons, explanations, examples, facts, and definitions. Lecturers often introduce supporting details with transitional phrases like the following:

Type of supporting detail	Transitional phrase
Reason	*A/The/One reason for this is/was that . . . / because . . .*
Explanation	*What I mean is . . . / In other words, . . .*
Example	*For instance/for example/like/such as . . .*
Fact	*In fact, . . . / Actually, . . .*
Definition	*By X, I mean . . . / X means . . .*

1 Read the following excerpts from the lecture. Predict which transitions from the box above the lecturer will use.

1 The four major groups that immigrated to the U.S. during this time were the Germans, the Irish, the Jews from Russia, and the Italians. Of course, there were many other immigrants – _____, from Poland, Greece, Hungary, China, and Mexico.

2 And all of them met with a lot of prejudice in this country. _____ prejudice, _____ that Americans did things _____ calling them cruel names or refusing to let them rent an apartment or give them a job.

3 Americans were worried about the size and diversity of the new foreign population. You have to remember that millions of immigrants arrived during this time, _____ almost 30 million of them.

4 Most people in the United States were Protestants, and they were often prejudiced against the Catholics and also against the Jews. _____ the immigrants' religious practices and traditions seemed strange to them.

5 The Irish, on the other hand, helped build the infrastructure of many American cities – _____, the canals, the bridges, the railroads, the seaports, and the roads.

2 Listen to the excerpts and fill in the blanks with the transitions you hear. ▶ **PLAY**

LECTURE, PART ONE: *Immigrants Face Prejudice*

GUESSING VOCABULARY FROM CONTEXT

1 The following items contain important vocabulary from Part One of the lecture. Work with a partner. Using the context and your knowledge of related words, take turns trying to guess the meanings of the words in **bold**.

_____ **1** Americans did things like calling [immigrants] **cruel** names . . .

_____ **2** Most of [the immigrants] **crowded** into cities . . .

_____ **3** I'm sure it was **frightening** for many Americans to see so many strangers moving into their cities.

_____ **4** Many Americans were afraid that the immigrants wouldn't share their **democratic values**.

_____ **5** People thought Germans living in America might be **unpatriotic**.

_____ **6** Immigrants were seen as a **threat** to the American way of life.

2 Work with a partner. Match the vocabulary terms with their definitions by writing the letter of each definition below in the blank next to the sentence containing the correct term in step 1. Check your answers in a dictionary if necessary.

  a hurtful, unfair
  b beliefs in democracy
  c large numbers moved into small spaces
  d danger
  e making people afraid or scared
  f not loyal to their country

🎧 NOTE TAKING: USING TELEGRAPHIC LANGUAGE

Telegraphic language consists mainly of words that convey information – nouns, verbs, adjectives, and adverbs. It usually does not include articles (*a*, *an*, and *the*) or the *be* verb. You have probably seen telegraphic language in newspaper headlines. When you take notes, you should use telegraphic language, abbreviations, and symbols to save time. For example:

You hear: *The four major groups that immigrated to the U.S. during this time were the Germans, the Irish, the Jews from Russia, and the Italians.*

You write: *4 maj grps imm'ed to U.S.: Germans, Irish, Jews (Russia), Italians.*

1 Look at the incomplete outline of Part One of Professor Meyer's lecture on the next page. Predict the kind of information you need to complete the notes.

Imms Face Prejudice

I. _____ :

    Germans, Irish, Jews (Russia), Italians

II. Prejudice

    Ex: _____, refuse to rent them apt. or give them

        jobs

III. _____

    A. _____ : 30 mill

    B. Diff relig

       ex: _____

    C. _____ + unfamiliar customs, foods, clothes, etc.

    D. People scared imms would not share democ. values

       ex: _____

    E. Amers. afraid of losing jobs

2   Now listen to Part One of the lecture. Fill in the blanks with the items below. Notice the use of telegraphic language, symbols, and abbreviations. ▶ **PLAY**

    Size of imm pop
    call imms cruel names
    prej vs Germans during WWI
    Reasons for prej
    prej vs Catholics + Jews
    4 maj imm grps imm'ed to U.S. @ this time
    Diff langs

3   Work with a partner and compare notes. Then use your notes to retell the information in Part One.

LECTURE, PART TWO: Immigrants Make Lasting Contributions

GUESSING VOCABULARY FROM CONTEXT

1 │ The following items contain important vocabulary from Part Two of the lecture. Work with a partner. Using the context and your knowledge of related words, take turns trying to guess the meanings of the words in **bold**.

     _____ **1** It was a time of great **expansion** in America.

     _____ **2** A lot of these new workers were immigrants who made many important and **lasting** contributions to the development of the country.

     _____ **3** They were good at farming and made important **improvements** to U.S. farming methods.

     _____ **4** [They] helped build the **infrastructure** of many American cities.

     _____ **5** Many were skilled workers, like **plumbers**.

     _____ **6** **There is no doubt** that all these immigrants made important contributions . . .

2 │ Work with your partner. Match the vocabulary terms with their definitions by writing the letter of each definition below in the blank next to the sentence containing the correct term in step 1. Check your answers in a dictionary if necessary.

    a positive developments
    b continuing for a long time
    c people who build systems of pipes that carry water
    d It is certain
    e growth
    f basic systems for transportation, communication, and energy

"Building of Brooklyn Bridge," New York City, 1882

☊ NOTE TAKING: ORGANIZING YOUR NOTES IN COLUMNS

> Organizing your notes in columns allows you to separate different types of information. For example, you can use columns to separate main ideas and supporting details, or you can decide to separate different categories of information based on your own ideas.

1 Look at these incomplete notes on Part Two of the lecture. They are divided into two columns, "Immigrant Groups" and "Examples of Contributions," based on the note-taker's ideas about how to take effective notes for this part of the lecture.

```
              Immigrants Make Lasting Contributions

   Immigrant Groups              Examples of Contributions

   _____    ⇨  _____, tailors, bakers, butchers

   Irish              ⇨  built _____
                         inc. skilled wkrs, e.g., _____
                         + unskilled, e.g., _____

   _____    ⇨  _____, entertainment, education,
                         science, _____  industry

   _____    ⇨  built _____, canals, _____,
                         buildings, and _____

   All imms           ⇨  Contrib to _____ and _____
                         e.g., _____, _____, music,
                         relig, lifestyles
```

2 Listen to Part Two of the lecture and fill in the blanks with the missing information. Remember to use symbols, abbreviations, and telegraphic language. ▶ **PLAY**

3 Work with a partner and compare notes. Then use your notes to retell the information in Part Two of the lecture.

AFTER THE LECTURE

ANSWERING MULTIPLE CHOICE QUESTIONS

Students are often required to take multiple choice tests. Because multiple choice questions are frequently graded by a computer, you must learn how to "bubble in" your response so that the circle you choose is completely filled. Here are some examples:

Correct   **Incorrect**   **Incorrect**

1 | Read the questions and bubble in the correct answer according to the information in the lecture. You may use your notes.

1 In the mid-nineteenth and early twentieth centuries, anti-immigrant feelings in the United States were _____.	**a** dangerous **b** common **c** unusual **d** rejected	○ a ○ b ○ c ○ d
2 How did most Americans view the immigrants?	**a** as welcome contributors **b** as a threat to the workers **c** as skilled competitors **d** as new friends	○ a ○ b ○ c ○ d
3 What was not a reason why Americans were afraid of the new foreign population?	**a** the newcomers adjusted quickly **b** they spoke other languages **c** their customs were different **d** they had different religions	○ a ○ b ○ c ○ d
4 What was the major religion in the United States at this time?	**a** Judaism **b** Protestantism **c** Catholicism **d** none	○ a ○ b ○ c ○ d
5 What was true about the newcomers?	**a** they contributed to the economy **b** they adopted Americans' lifestyles **c** they spoke only to each other **d** they learned English quickly	○ a ○ b ○ c ○ d
6 Why were there many new jobs in America?	**a** because of World War I **b** because of foreign immigration **c** because of the growth of industry **d** because of World War II	○ a ○ b ○ c ○ d

2 | Work with a partner and compare answers.

Chapter 4

Diversity in Today's United States

1 GETTING STARTED

In this section, you are going to read about immigration to the United States from the second half of the twentieth century until the present. You will also hear statistics about this immigration and examine graphs about recent immigrants' countries of origin.

READING AND THINKING ABOUT THE TOPIC

1 | Read the following passage.

In 1965, there was a major change in U.S. immigration laws, and the number of people allowed to come into the United States began to increase. The pattern of immigration also changed. A century ago, the majority of immigrants came from Europe. Since 1965, most immigrants have come from Latin America and Asia. Nowadays they arrive from countries such as Mexico, China, and India, and from the Caribbean and eastern Europe. With so many ethnic groups, religions, and races, the United States is now one of the most diverse nations on earth.

Economic opportunity and political freedom are still the main reasons why immigrants come to this country, but other factors are important, too. Americans' acceptance of diversity, better educational opportunities, and the existence of health care are other reasons why immigrants choose to make the United States their home.

Today's immigrants differ from one another in many ways. For example, some come to join their families, while others leave their families behind. Some immigrants are poor, uneducated workers, and others are middle-class professionals. After arriving in the United States, some make a lot of money, while others remain poor. Finally, there are differences in the way immigrants adapt to American society. Some adapt completely to the new culture and think of themselves as *American*. Others feel that they are a combination of both their original and new cultures. These immigrants sometimes call themselves *hyphenated Americans* (for example, "Mexican-American" or "Chinese-American"). Still others keep their original culture for their whole life.

2 Answer the following questions according to the information in the passage:
  1 How have immigration patterns to the United States changed since 1965?
  2 Why do immigrants continue to come to America?
  3 In what ways are immigrants different from each other?

3 Read these questions and share your answers with a partner.
  1 Do you know any people who have immigrated to the United States since 1965? Why did they immigrate? Did they adapt to American society successfully?
  2 Why do you think immigrants sometimes adapt in different ways?

⌒ LISTENING FOR PERCENTAGES AND FRACTIONS

Percentages and fractions are commonly used in academic courses. They can be used for different purposes, such as explaining a graph or giving an example.

To express percentages, just add *percent* to a number. For example:
  "1%" is said as *one percent*
  "3%" is said as *three percent*
  "13%" is said as *thirteen percent*
  "30%" is said as *thirty percent*
  "32%" is said as *thirty-two percent*
  "100%" is said as *one hundred percent*

Fractions are expressed in the following ways:
  "1/2" is said as *half* or *one-half* or *a half*
  "1/3" is said as *one-third* or *a third*
  "1/4" is said as *one-quarter* or *one-fourth* or *a quarter* or *a fourth*
  "3/4" is said as *three-quarters* or *three-fourths*

1 Study the three pie charts below. They show legal immigration to the United States in the twentieth century.

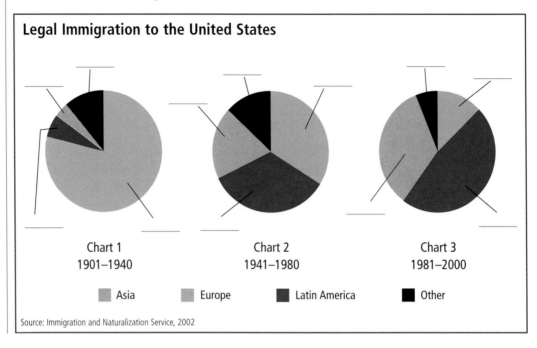

Legal Immigration to the United States

Chart 1
1901–1940

Chart 2
1941–1980

Chart 3
1981–2000

Asia   Europe   Latin America   Other

Source: Immigration and Naturalization Service, 2002

2 Discuss these questions about the pie charts with a partner:
   1 Which time periods are shown?
   2 Which parts of the world are included?
   3 What percentages or fractions do you predict you might hear?

3 Listen to a description of twentieth-century immigration patterns. As you listen, fill in the blanks next to each pie chart with the percentages you hear. ▶ **PLAY**

4 Work with a partner and compare your answers. Then discuss the following questions:
   1 Since 1901, what has happened to the percentage of immigrants from Europe, Latin America, and Asia?
   2 What fraction or percentage of immigrants came from Europe, Latin America, Asia, and other places between 1981 and 2000?
   3 How do you think immigration patterns might change in the future? Why?

2 AMERICAN VOICES: Agustín, Nadezhda, Chao, Alvin, Minsoo, and Abdoul-Aziz

In this section, you will hear interviews with six immigrants to the United States. First, Agustín, Nadezhda, and Chao will discuss their reasons for coming to the United States. Then Alvin, Minsoo, and Abdoul-Aziz will talk about adapting to life in this country.

BEFORE THE INTERVIEWS

SHARING YOUR OPINION

1 | Imagine that you are an immigrant to the United States. What were your reasons for coming to this country? Mark each item below as: *1* (very important), *2* (important), or *3* (not very important).

_____ The opportunity to make money   _____ Equal rights for women

_____ A good health care system   _____ A democratic government

_____ A good educational system   _____ A safe place to raise children

_____ A diverse culture   _____ Other (your own ideas)

2 | Work in small groups. Discuss your answers to step 1.

BUILDING BACKGROUND KNOWLEDGE

1 | Read the following passage.

In 2003, the organization Public Agenda interviewed more than 1,000 immigrants to the United States from about 100 countries. The immigrants were asked if they agreed with statements like the following:

_____ **1** I have become an American.

_____ **2** I act like an American outside, but at home I keep my own culture and traditions.

_____ **3** I phone family or friends in my home country a few times a month.

_____ **4** My children [under 18] probably will not want to return to my country to live.

_____ **5** The most important thing about living in the United States is having freedom to live my life the way I choose.

_____ **6** Speaking English is the key to success in America.

_____ **7** I would come to America again if I could go back in time.

2 | Work with a partner. From the list below, guess the percentage of immigrants who agreed with the statements above and write the letters in the blanks in step 1.
a 80   **b** 42   **c** 41   **d** 59   **e** 70   **f** 40   **g** 87

3 | Check your answers to step 2 at the bottom of page 59. Then discuss them with a partner.

INTERVIEW WITH AGUSTIN, NADEZHDA, AND CHAO: Reasons for coming to the United States

Here are some words and phrases from the interview printed in **bold** and given in the context in which you will hear them. They are followed by definitions.

I was washing dishes, but I didn't want to **get stuck** doing that: *do something forever*

We're often in contact. I always send money and **presents** back home: *We communicate often / gifts*

I **made a sacrifice** for my children: *left something that was important to me*

I want to become a **physician's assistant**: *a person trained to help a doctor*

I work in a **tofu** factory: *soybean cake (a common food in parts of Asia)*

I'm studying to make my dream **come true**: *happen, become real*

⌒ LISTENING FOR SPECIFIC INFORMATION

1 Look at the chart below and notice the information you need to listen for in the interviews with Agustín, Nadezhda, and Chao.

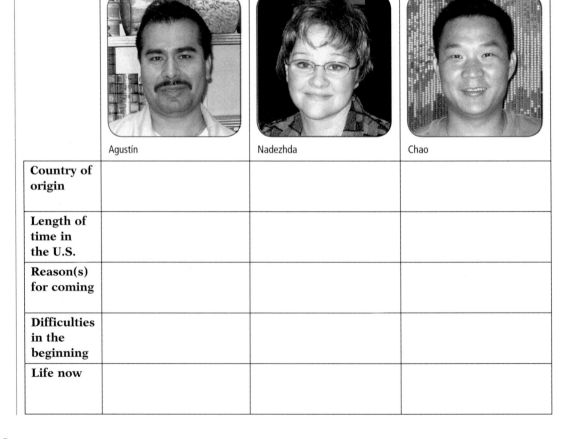

	Agustín	Nadezhda	Chao
Country of origin			
Length of time in the U.S.			
Reason(s) for coming			
Difficulties in the beginning			
Life now			

2 Listen to the interviews and fill in the chart with the information you hear. ▶ PLAY

3 Work with a partner and compare answers. Then discuss the following questions:

  1 How are the speakers' experiences similar? How are they different?

  2 What were the hardest experiences the speakers had?

INTERVIEW WITH ALVIN, MINSOO, AND ABDOUL-AZIZ: Adapting to life in the United States

Here are some words and phrases from the interview printed in **bold** and given in the context in which you will hear them. They are followed by definitions.

I think I'm a **hybrid**, because I'm a combination of two cultures: *a thing made by combining parts from two different sources*

Whenever I **step outside the door**, I **step** into a different world: *leave my house / walk*

I'm constantly going **back and forth** between the two cultures: *from one to the other*

I'm **not used to** giving my opinion in class: *not something I usually do, not a habit*

I'm **absorbing** American culture fast: *getting familiar with, taking in*

Isn't it hard for you to **keep switching** languages?: *change all the time*

Am I a **mixture** of both?: *combination*

I'm not as **formal** as I used to be: *correct, serious, extremely polite*

🎧 LISTENING FOR SPECIFIC INFORMATION

1 Before you listen to the interview, read the paragraphs summarizing the conversations with Alvin, Minsoo, and Abdoul-Aziz. Predict the kind of information you need to listen for.

Alvin	Alvin's family is from _____, but he grew up in _____. He describes himself as a _____, which is a combination of two cultures. He says he is _____ on the outside and _____ inside. At home, he always speaks _____, listens to _____, and eats _____ food. When he goes outside, he says he feels as if he is stepping into a different _____, so he is constantly going _____ between two cultures.
Minsoo	Minsoo is from _____, and she came to the United States five years ago. At home, she speaks _____. She only speaks English at _____ and in college. It is difficult for her at college, because she is not used to giving her _____ in class. Minsoo feels that she is half _____ and half American, but she says she is _____ American culture fast.

Abdoul-Aziz grew up in _____ and came to the United States as an _____. He speaks three languages: _____ at work and school, _____ with some of his friends, and Hausa, an _____ language, with _____. He says it is hard to keep _____ languages because it feels like he is constantly changing his _____. He often asks himself: Am I African? Am I American? Or am I a _____ of both?

Abdoul-Aziz

2 | Listen to the interviews. As you listen, fill in the blanks in the paragraphs. Then work with a partner and compare answers. **▶ PLAY**

3 | Work with a partner. Choose two people from the interviews and role-play a conversation between them. You can use questions like these to begin:

1 Why did you come to the United States?
2 What exciting, frightening, or difficult experience did you have when you first arrived?
3 Do you miss your home country? If so, in what ways?
4 Do you think of yourself as an American?

AFTER THE INTERVIEWS

SHARING YOUR KNOWLEDGE

Work with a partner. Ask and answer the chain of questions in the chart below. Use examples and stories to tell about your experiences. Begin here:

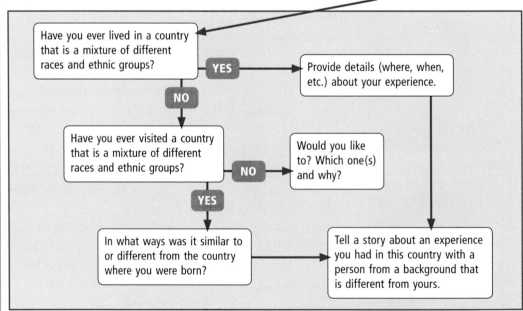

3 IN YOUR OWN VOICE

When you think of American food, what dishes do you think of? Hot dogs and hamburgers? In fact, you can find almost every kind of food in the United States because U.S. culture is so diverse. In this section, you will give a short oral presentation about a dish that was brought to America by an immigrant group but is now considered part of American cooking.

GIVING AN ORAL PRESENTATION

Here are some guidelines for preparing and giving oral presentations:

- Plan your presentation carefully. It is usually not necessary to write and memorize every word you will say. Instead, you can make notes or write an outline of your talk on index cards.
- Look up the pronunciation of new or difficult vocabulary in a dictionary.
- Practice your presentation out loud in front of a mirror or with a friend. Use the notes you have prepared.
- During your presentation in class, speak loudly and clearly. Make frequent eye contact with your audience.
- Use pictures or objects to make your presentation more interesting.

1 | Work with a partner. Read the list of dishes below and match each one with the country or region it originally came from.

_____	1 sushi	a Jamaica
_____	2 tacos	b China
_____	3 hummus	c Japan
_____	4 gyros	d Mexico
_____	5 samosas	e Middle East
_____	6 ackee	f Eastern Europe
_____	7 egg drop soup	g Italy
_____	8 matzo ball soup	h Germany
_____	9 pizza	i Greece
_____	10 hot dogs	j India

2 | Choose one of the dishes from step 1 and prepare a three-to-five-minute oral presentation about it. You may also choose a dish that is not on the list. Include the answers to the following questions in your presentation:

1 What is the name of the dish, and what country did it come from originally?

2 What ingredients does it contain?

3 How do you prepare it?

4 What does it look like when it is finished?

5 What other foods can you eat with this dish?

4 ACADEMIC LISTENING AND NOTE TAKING: Recent Immigrants and Today's United States

In this section, you will hear and take notes on a two-part lecture by Betty Jordan, a professor of U.S. history. The title of her lecture is *Recent Immigrants and Today's United States*. Professor Jordan will talk about models, or metaphors, for describing America's diverse immigrant society. She will also discuss *transnationalism,* a word that describes recent immigrants' continuing relationships with their home countries.

BEFORE THE LECTURE

PREVIEWING THE TOPIC

1 Work with a partner. Look at the PowerPoint slides from the speaker's presentation.

*The art on the cover of this book is a patchwork quilt. Read about it in the photographic and illustration credits on page 162.

2 Complete the following sentence and explain your answer to your partner:

I think the United States is most like picture _____ because . . .

3 Imagine that you have recently immigrated to another country. Look at the activities below and check the column that describes how often you would do each one.

I would . . .	Very often	Often	Sometimes	Almost never
Phone people in my home country				
Communicate online with family and friends back home				
Celebrate traditional holidays from my home country				
Cook food from my home country				
Follow sports events in my home country				
Speak my native language with my children				
Speak my native language with other people from my home country				
Practice my religion				
Send money to people in my home country				
Visit my home country				

4 Work in small groups and discuss these questions: What kind of immigrant would you be, based on your answers to step 3? Would you completely adapt to your new culture, adapt in some ways but not others, or not adapt at all?

🎧 NOTE TAKING: LISTENING FOR DEFINITIONS

Good lecturers usually define important terms and difficult vocabulary. Definitions often follow this formula:

X (*word being defined*) is a (*category or type of something*) that/who/where (*details*)

For example,

- An *immigrant* is a person who goes to live in another country.
- *Transnationalism* is a word that describes recent immigrants' relationships with their home countries.

1 Work with a partner. Draw lines from column to column to create complete definitions. Follow the example.

Word	is a(n) . . .	details
1 A metaphor	toy	that is used to help us understand things that are very complex, like societies.
2 A melting pot	cover for a bed	that is used for melting things, such as different foods.
3 A salad	image, a picture, or a model	made of different vegetables that are mixed together.
4 A patchwork quilt	dish	and it's made from colorful pieces of cloth sewn together.
5 A kaleidoscope	large metal pot, a kind of container	that you look through, and if you turn it, you can see beautiful, changing patterns.

2 Listen to the definitions and check your answers. ▶ **PLAY**

LECTURE, PART ONE: Metaphors for Describing American Society

GUESSING VOCABULARY FROM CONTEXT

1 The following items contain important vocabulary from Part One of the lecture. Work with a partner. Using the context and your knowledge of related words, take turns trying to guess the meanings of the words in **bold**.

Answers to "Building Background Knowledge," step 2, page 53:
1 b 2 c 3 d 4 e 5 f 6 g 7 a

_____ 1 The ingredients all **melt** together and become something new.

_____ 2 A fondue . . . [is] a dish from Switzerland that has cheese and other **ingredients**.

_____ 3 Many immigrants keep parts of their own cultural **identity**.

_____ 4 They may **celebrate** their own traditional holidays.

_____ 5 They usually marry someone from their own race, their own **ethnic** group.

_____ 6 . . . pieces of colorful cloth **sewn** together.

_____ 7 This is the metaphor I like best because it's very **dynamic**.

_____ 8 It shows America as a beautiful picture – a **multiracial**, **multiethnic**, **multicultural** society.

2 │ Work with a partner. Match the vocabulary terms with their definitions by writing the letter of each definition below in the blank next to the sentence containing the correct term in step 1. Check your answers in a dictionary if necessary.

  a composed of many races, ethnic groups, and cultures
  b always moving or changing
  c items of food that are used in cooking or preparing a dish
  d people's idea of who they are and what makes them special
  e enjoy a special event, such as a holiday, by eating and drinking, playing special music, or participating in traditional activities
  f made by sewing, using a needle and thread
  g relating to a particular race, nationality, or culture
  h change from a solid to a liquid form because they are heated

◖ NOTE TAKING: USING NUMBERS TO ORGANIZE YOUR NOTES

An easy way to organize your notes is to use numbers to list main ideas or details. Using numbers together with symbols, abbreviations, and telegraphic language allows you to take notes quickly.

For example, you hear:

Over the years, historians and writers have used different metaphors to try to describe this complex American culture, and what I'd like to do today is first to describe four of those metaphors to you. Then, in the second part of the lecture, I'll talk about transnationalism, _a word that describes the relationship that recent immigrants continue to have with their home countries._

Your notes could look like this:

Topic of lec: _____
   1. Metaphors for describing American culture
   2. Transnationalism – r'ship of imms w/ home country

1 Look at these notes for Part One of the lecture. Notice how the note taker has used numbers to identify and organize the main ideas. Predict the information you will need to listen for.

Metaphors for descr. Am. society:

1. Melting pot = pot used for melting foods, etc.

   Ingredients melt together & become someth. new, e.g., fondue

   Acc. to metaphor, imms to U.S. would lose separate ID & mix w/ people here.

   Problem w/ metaphor: doesn't describe today's reality, i.e.,
      many imms aren't accepted
      many imms keep parts of their own ID — lang, traditions, marry from same
         ethnic grp, never say they are American.

2. Salad bowl

   Salad = _____

   Metaphor represents America as _____

   _____

3. _____ = _____.

   Made of _____

   People like metaphor because _____

4. _____.

   _____

2 Now listen to Part One of the lecture and complete the notes. ▶ PLAY

3 Work with a partner and compare notes. Use them to retell the information in Part One.

4 Think of your own metaphor for American society and explain it to your partner by completing the following sentence:

America is a(n) _____ because . . .

LECTURE, PART TWO: *Transnationalism*

GUESSING VOCABULARY FROM CONTEXT

1 The following items contain important vocabulary from Part Two of the lecture. Work with a partner. Using the context and your knowledge of related words, take turns trying to guess the meanings of the words in **bold**.

_____ **1** Today's immigrants often keep parts of their own cultural identity at the same time as they become part of **mainstream** American society.

_____ **2** Today's immigrants also **maintain** some kind of relationship with their countries of origin.

_____ **3** Many immigrants **own** homes, land, or businesses in their country of origin.

_____ **4** There are different factors that make this possible, like **ease** of travel and technology.

_____ **5** People can go back and forth between the U.S. and their **homeland** more often.

_____ **6** Communication technology has **advanced**, too . . .

2 Work with your partner. Match the vocabulary terms with their definitions by writing the letter of each definition below in the blank next to the sentence containing the correct term in step 1. Check your answers in a dictionary if necessary.

a made progress
b have, possess
c keep, have
d without difficulty
e country of origin, home country
f way of life or beliefs accepted by most people

🎧 NOTE TAKING: USING BULLETS TO ORGANIZE YOUR NOTES

Bullets are a useful technique for marking lists of details. You can use them with numbers or instead of numbers. For example, you hear:

Now why do you think immigrants today have a closer relationship with their home countries than they did in the past? Well, there are different factors that make this possible, like ease of travel and technology . . .

Your notes could look like this:

Imm's have close r'ship w/home countries - why?
- travel
- technology

1 | Look at these notes on Part Two of the lecture and notice how the note taker has used bullets, together with numbers, to help identify and organize the main ideas and examples.

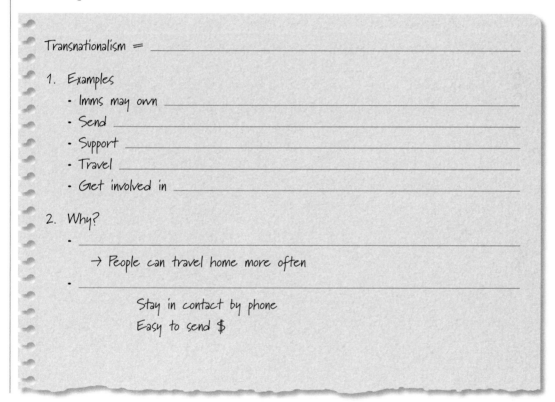

Transnationalism = _____

1. Examples
   - Imms may own _____
   - Send _____
   - Support _____
   - Travel _____
   - Get involved in _____

2. Why?
   - _____
     → People can travel home more often
   - _____
         Stay in contact by phone
         Easy to send $

2 | Listen to Part Two of the lecture and complete the notes. ▶ PLAY

3 | Work with a partner and compare your notes. Use them to retell the information in Part Two.

AFTER THE LECTURE

SHARING YOUR OPINION

1 | Read the postcards that Jo Ann, who is from England, sent to her friend Sharon in their hometown of Basildon.

> Sharon – Just a quick note to tell you I've arrived safely in Southern California. I like my college a lot, and I've got a great roommate, Maria (she's from New Mexico). What's amazing is how much there is to do here even though the town is small. There's a Native American arts center near the college, and right on my block there's a Russian dance studio where they give free performances Friday nights. Plus lots of fun places to eat – last night a few of us went to a terrific Turkish restaurant that has live music.
>
> Gotta go. Will try to write more later.
>
> xxx
>
> Jo Ann

> TO:
> Sharon Davis
> P.O. Box 1904
> Essex
> SS16 1ZQ
> UK

> Hi Sharon,
> I'm having a great time in New York! Too bad spring break is so short. Can you believe that there's a Chinese, a Jamaican, a Lebanese, a Mexican, an Italian & a Japanese restaurant all on the same street?? And the choice of music is amazing: jazz, swing, classical, rock, hip-hop. I've never seen anything like it! Yesterday, Maria and I went to Queens – it's just across the East River – & we walked through an Indian neighborhood and then a Mexican one. And then we went to a museum that had all kinds of contemporary art. I'm taking lots of photos. Will send them as soon as I get back to CA.
>   Love – Jo Ann

> TO:
> Sharon Davis
> P.O. Box 1904
> ESSEX
> SS16 1ZQ
> UK

2 | Discuss the following questions with a partner:

1 Where is Jo Ann, and what is she doing?

2 What does her description tell you about life in the United States? How does it support what you have learned in this unit?

The Struggle for Equality

This unit is about the struggle for equality in the United States. Equality was an important ideal for the men who founded the country, but in the early days of U.S. history, everyone did not have the same rights or opportunities. For example, only white men who owned property could vote. Chapter 5 is about political movements in the nineteenth and twentieth centuries that led to greater equality for African Americans and for women. You will hear interviews with two women who experienced discrimination, that is, unfair or illegal treatment because of a particular quality such as color, gender, or age. You will also listen to a lecture on the civil rights movement and the women's movement. Chapter 6 discusses progress that has been made since the 1960s. You will listen to people talk about groups that have made progress toward greater equality, and you will hear a lecture about laws that have advanced America's struggle for equality.

The Struggle Begins

Chapter 5

The word *colored* was commonly used for African Americans until the 1960s.

1 GETTING STARTED

In this section, you will read background information about the inequalities that African Americans and women faced from the middle of the nineteenth century until the middle of the twentieth. As you read, notice that the terms *African Americans* and *blacks* are often used interchangeably.

READING AND THINKING ABOUT THE TOPIC

1 | Read the following passage.

> The Civil War between the North and the South (1861–1865) resulted in a major step forward in the struggle for equality of African Americans in America. At the end of the war, Congress passed the Thirteenth Amendment to the Constitution, which freed all slaves. A short time later, the Fourteenth Amendment was passed, which promised "equal protection of the laws" to all citizens. And then in 1870, the Fifteenth Amendment gave African-American men the right to vote. However, in the following decades, laws in the South called "Jim Crow*" laws continued to limit the rights of black Americans. For example, blacks were not allowed to study in the same schools as whites, they were forced to sit at the back of buses, and they had to use separate bathrooms and water fountains. In 1954, the Supreme Court decided that segregation, that is, the forced separation of the races, was illegal in public schools, but it took many more years of struggle before the Jim Crow laws were completely reversed.
>
> ---
> * Jim Crow was the name a popular white comic actor used when he played the character of a poor, uneducated black man. He played the role in a way that made Jim Crow seem stupid.

American women also began their struggle for equality around the time of the Civil War. Although many women had supported freeing the slaves and giving equal rights to blacks, they did not have many legal rights either. For example, they could not vote, they could not own land without their husbands' permission, and they usually depended on their husbands or male relatives for economic support. It wasn't until 1920, with the passage of the Nineteenth Amendment, that women finally won the right to vote. During World War II (1939–1945), many women worked outside their homes for the first time. This was also an important step forward in their struggle for equal rights.

In the 1960s, both African Americans and women gained important rights. The Equal Pay Act, a law passed in 1963, legalized equal pay for men and women. The Civil Rights Act, a law passed in 1964, made it illegal to discriminate against workers because of their race or gender. However, inequalities still existed.

2 | Answer the following questions according to the information in the passage:

1 Which events between the mid-nineteenth and mid-twentieth centuries led to greater equality for African Americans?

2 How did women's rights change during this time?

3 What laws were passed in the 1960s? How did they help blacks and women?

3 | Read these questions and share your responses with a partner:

1 What does equality mean to you?

2 Do you know of any laws that guarantee equal pay in other countries? Do you know when and why they were passed?

🎧 BUILDING BACKGROUND KNOWLEDGE

1 | Work with a partner. Look at the photos and read the captions under them. Predict the order in which the events happened.

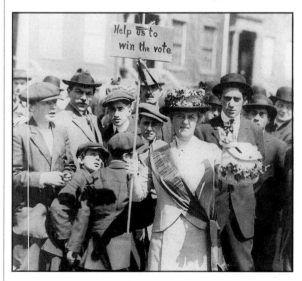

a _____ After decades of protest, women finally won the right to vote when the Nineteenth Amendment passed.

b _____ The Declaration of Independence was adopted in Philadelphia, Pennsylvania. It included the words "all men are created equal."

c _____ After years of protest against segregated schools, the Supreme Court ended legal segregation of public schools in a case called *Brown versus Board of Education of Topeka [Kansas]*.

d _____ Jim Crow laws were in effect in the American South.

Lucretia Mott (left)
Elizabeth Cady
Stanton (right)

e _____ The first Women's Rights Convention was held in the town of Seneca Falls, New York. Women demanded the right to vote and equality with men.

f _____ The Civil War ended and the Thirteenth Amendment was passed. This amendment ended slavery.

2 Listen to information about the pictures. Fill in the blanks with the dates you hear. Then compare the order of the events with your predictions in step 1. ▶ **PLAY**

2 AMERICAN VOICES: Cynthia and Hilda

In this section, you will hear two women tell stories about their experiences with inequality. First, you will listen to Cynthia, who is African American, talk about an event from her life before the civil rights movement. Then you will hear Hilda, a retired teacher, talk about progress toward women's rights from the 1950s until today.

BEFORE THE INTERVIEWS

BUILDING BACKGROUND KNOWLEDGE

1 From the 1880s until the 1960s, many American states, especially in the South, practiced segregation. Read the following statements and guess if they are true or false. Write *T* (true) or *F* (false) in the blanks.

_____ **1 Alabama**: Restaurants would not serve whites and blacks in the same parts of the restaurant.

_____ **2 Florida**: Blacks were not allowed to marry whites.

_____ **3 Georgia**: Black children were not allowed to play ball games within ten blocks of a white baseball team.

_____ **4 Mississippi**: A person who was one-quarter black could not marry a white person.

_____ **5 North Carolina**: A textbook used by a black child could not be used by a white child.

_____ **6 Oklahoma**: There were separate telephone booths for whites and blacks.

2 Until the women's movement in the 1960s, women did not have the same rights as men. Read the following statements and guess if they are true or false. Write *T* (true) or *F* (false) in the blanks.

_____ **1** In the late nineteenth century, most poor women did not learn how to read or write.

_____ **2** In the late nineteenth century, the U.S. Supreme Court ruled that married women could not become lawyers.

_____ **3** Elizabeth Blackwell, who received her medical degree in 1849, was the first woman in the United States to become a doctor.

_____ **4** Until the 1960s, employers could refuse to give a job to a pregnant woman.

_____ **5** In 2005, American women earned an average of 79 cents for every dollar earned by men.

_____ **6** In 2005, 14 out of 100 U.S. senators were women.

3 Check your answers to steps 1 and 2 at the bottom of page 73. Then tell your classmates which fact surprised you the most.

INTERVIEW WITH CYNTHIA: *Before the civil rights movement*

Here are some words and phrases from the interview with Cynthia printed in **bold** and given in the context in which you will hear them. They are followed by definitions.

[We'd take a trip] to **reconnect** with the family down there: *see them again*

Were you aware of segregation in the South?: *Did you know about*

The owner . . . **grabbed me**: *took hold of me in a strong way*

He **swung me around**: *picked me up and turned me around*

I was really **startled**: *very surprised, shocked*

My father still doesn't want to talk about . . . how **helpless** he felt: *without power*

Although we see progress, . . . there are still **challenges**: *difficulties*

Cynthia

🎧 LISTENING FOR ANSWERS TO *WH*-QUESTIONS

When speakers tell stories about events that happened to them, they often include the answers to *Wh*-questions:

- WHO (was involved)?
- WHAT (happened to them)?
- WHEN (did the event happen)?
- WHERE (did it happen)?
- WHY or HOW (did it happen)?

Listening for answers to these questions will help you understand the point the speaker is making.

1 | Before you listen to the interview, read the following *Wh*-questions about the experience Cynthia describes:

1 Who was Cynthia with when she had this experience?
2 What happened to her?
3 When did this experience take place?
4 Where was the family going?
5 Why was the event so frightening?

2 | Now listen to the interview and take notes on the answers to the questions in step 1.
▶ PLAY

3 | Compare your answers with a partner.

INTERVIEW WITH HILDA: Before and after the women's movement

> Here are some words and phrases from the interview with Hilda printed in **bold** and given in the context in which you will hear them. They are followed by definitions.
>
> Since I was born, incredible changes have **come about**: *happened*
>
> You don't need a college education to change **diapers**: *babies' underclothes*
>
> It took a while until I **realized** that I could do even better than that: *became aware*
>
> It was **phenomenal**: *fantastic, wonderful*
>
> Those kinds of **demands** opened my eyes: *strong requests*
>
> I can get an education and **make something of myself**: *become successful*
>
> Back then, that was a **big deal**: *something important*

Hilda

🎧 LISTENING FOR SPECIFIC INFORMATION

1 Read the questions below before you listen to the interview with Hilda.

1 In what decade did Hilda go to high school?
  a 1940s
  b 1950s
  c 1960s

2 How many children did the "typical" American family have at that time?
  a one
  b two
  c four

3 Who went to college in Hilda's family?
  a her father
  b her mother
  c her brother

4 What was Hilda's dream?
  a to be a secretary
  b to go to college
  c to be a housewife

5 What did Hilda do after the 1965 women's demonstration in Chicago?
  a She married her brother's friend.
  b She went to college.
  c She got her first job.

6 What does Hilda think of the situation of women today?
  a It has not changed.
  b It is better than before.
  c It is worse than ever.

2 Now listen to the interview and circle the answers to the questions. **▶ PLAY**

3 Work with a partner and check your answers. Then compare Hilda's life with the life of a woman you know well who is about Hilda's age.

AFTER THE INTERVIEWS

DRAWING INFERENCES

Drawing inferences, sometimes called "reading between the lines," means understanding information that speakers do not say directly. In order to draw inferences, you must use your background knowledge, the speaker's tone of voice, and context clues to reach logical conclusions.

1 Work with a partner and discuss the following inference questions:
1. How did Cynthia and her family members probably feel after the experience at the gas station?
2. Why do you think Cynthia's father did not want to discuss the experience?
3. How do you think Hilda's family felt about her career choices?
4. How do you think Hilda's life would be different if she were a young woman today?

2 Imagine that it is the day after Cynthia's experience at the gas station or that it is the day after Hilda's experience at the women's demonstration. Write an imaginary diary entry by either Cynthia or Hilda. Then read your diary entry to a partner or a small group. (Use your own paper if you need more space.)

Answers to "Building Background Knowledge," steps 1 and 2, page 70:
Step 1: All statements are true except 3 (2 blocks, not 10) and 4 (one-eighth, not one-quarter).
Step 2: All statements are true except 5 (87 cents, not 79 cents).

3 IN YOUR OWN VOICE

In this section, you will do research about people who are famous for their contributions to the struggle for equality of African Americans or women. Then you will give an oral presentation on your research.

CONDUCTING RESEARCH

1 | Work in groups. Each group will do research on a different person from the following list:

- Susan B. Anthony
- Stokely Carmichael
- George Washington Carver
- Frederick Douglass
- Betty Friedan
- Lyndon Johnson
- Martin Luther King, Jr.
- Lucretia Mott
- Rosa Parks
- Elizabeth Cady Stanton
- Gloria Steinem
- Malcolm X

2 | Using Internet sources or a library, try to find the following information:

- Date and place of birth and/or death
- Details about the person's life
- A photograph
- Most important contributions

GIVING AN ORAL PRESENTATION

1 | As a group, prepare a short presentation on the person you have researched. Decide which students in your group will present which parts of the information you found. Practice your presentation out loud at least once. If you wish, you can make a poster to display the photograph and any other interesting visual information that you found.

2 | Give your presentation to the class. After the presentation, take turns answering your classmates' questions and responding to their comments.

RESPONDING TO PRESENTATIONS

Speakers usually reserve time for listeners to ask questions at the end of their presentations. Always pay close attention to a presentation so that you will be prepared to ask questions. You can:

- Ask the speaker(s) to repeat or explain something you did not understand.
- Ask for more information about the topic of the presentation.
- Make a comment on what you heard.

1 | Listen to your classmates' presentations and take notes. Write at least one question you would like to ask the presenters or one comment you would like to make.

2 | Following each presentation, raise your hand and prepare to ask your question or share your comment. Listen to other students' questions and comments and the presenters' answers. Add to your notes any new information that you hear.

4 ACADEMIC LISTENING AND NOTE TAKING: The Civil Rights Movement and the Women's Movement

In this section, you will hear and take notes on a two-part lecture by Julia Smith, a former professor of anthropology. The title of her lecture is *The Civil Rights Movement and the Women's Movement.* Professor Smith will discuss these two important political movements of the mid-twentieth century and explain how they changed the United States.

BEFORE THE LECTURE

BUILDING BACKGROUND KNOWLEDGE

Work with a partner. Look at the pictures and discuss the following questions:

1 Who are the people in the pictures? What are they doing?

2 Do the people in the two photos want the same things?

3 When do you think these pictures were taken?

🎧 NOTE TAKING: LISTENING FOR GUIDING QUESTIONS

Lecturers often use guiding questions, also called *rhetorical questions,* to introduce main ideas or important details. Lecturers normally answer such questions themselves. You should take notes on the questions and the answers. For example:

The lecturer says:

What was the civil rights movement? Well, the civil rights movement was the struggle by hundreds of thousands of people to achieve equal rights for African Americans.

You write:

Civ rights movt = ?

   Strug. by 100,000s of people to achieve eq rts. for Af. Am's

1 In the left column below, you will see the guiding questions that the lecturer asks. Read the questions and match them with answers from the column on the right.

Guiding Questions	Answers
_____ **1** So, these are just a few examples of important events in the early struggle for civil rights. What happened next?	**a** Well, first the Jim Crow laws were overturned.
_____ **2** Today we can look back and be thankful for the great achievements of the civil rights movement. What were some of these achievements?	**b** Well, these events led to more protests, more demonstrations, and more sit-ins throughout the 60s.
_____ **3** A journalist named Betty Friedan* published a book called *The Feminine Mystique*. It was based on interviews with white, middle-class women living in the suburbs, and what do you think Friedan discovered?	**c** In some ways yes, of course. Today "equal pay for equal work" is the law.
_____ **4** Was the women's movement successful?	**d** That these women were very unhappy with their lives, with their lack of freedom, and lack of a sense of identity.

2 Now listen to the questions and answers and check to see if you matched them correctly. ▶ **PLAY**

LECTURE, PART ONE: The Civil Rights Movement

GUESSING VOCABULARY FROM CONTEXT

1 The following items contain important vocabulary from Part One of the lecture. Work with a partner. Using the context and your knowledge of related words, take turns trying to guess the meanings of the words in **bold**.

_____ **1** [At that time] there were many political and social **movements**.

_____ **2** [These movements] **involved** thousands of people all over the nation.

_____ **3** [These movements] **led to** new laws.

_____ **4** [The civil rights movement was] the struggle by hundreds of thousands of people . . . to **achieve** equal rights for African Americans.

_____ **5** There were several **key** historical events.

_____ **6** This [event] led to the famous Montgomery bus **boycott**.

_____ **7** The Jim Crow laws were **overturned**.

---

* In the right-hand photograph on page 75, Betty Friedan is the woman at the front of the line.

2 Work with your partner. Match the vocabulary terms with their definitions by writing the letter of each definition below in the blank next to the sentence or phrase containing the correct term in step 1. Check your answers in a dictionary if necessary.

    a caused (something) to happen
    b extremely important
    c get, gain
    d groups of people with the same ideas working together for a goal
    e made illegal
    f refusing to buy a product or use a service as a way of showing strong disapproval
    g included

NOTE TAKING: CREATING YOUR OWN SYMBOLS AND ABBREVIATIONS

> In Chapter 2, you learned some common symbols and abbreviations to use in note taking. You must also get in the habit of developing your own symbols and abbreviations for words you hear in lectures.

1 Work with a partner. Read the following list of key words and expressions from the lecture and create your own symbols or abbreviations for them.

Key Word or Expression	Symbol or Abbreviation	Key Word or Expression	Symbol or Abbreviation
a African Americans		**i** movement	
b black		**j** opportunities	
c civil rights movement		**k** rights	
d demonstration		**l** segregation	
e education		**m** students	
f equal, equality		**n** thousands	
g inequality		**o** women	
h Martin Luther King, Jr.		**p** women's movement	

2 Read the notes from Part One of Julia Smith's lecture. Notice that the note taker used columns to record the guiding questions and matching answers. Some of the information is missing. Predict the kind of information you need to listen for.

Pt. 1: The _____

What was it?   Strug. by _____ of people to achieve
                _____ for _____

How did it start? 100 yrs. after end of slav., _____ still common
                   → beg. of _____.

Key events: 1. Dec 1, 1955: Rosa Parks _____
                    _____ → Montgomery bus _____

                2. 1960: blk sts refused _____
                    _____ = _____

                3. March 1963: March on _____
                    _____ people heard _____
                    give "I Have a Dream" speech.

_____ ? More _____
                    _____

_____ ? 1. Jim Crow laws overturned
                    2. Fed. gov't passed laws _____
                    3. _____

3 | Now listen to Part One of the lecture and complete the notes. Include your symbols and abbreviations from step 1. ▶ PLAY

4 | Work with a partner and compare your notes. Then use them to review the guiding questions and matching answers.

LECTURE, PART TWO: The Women's Movement

GUESSING VOCABULARY FROM CONTEXT

1 | The following items contain important vocabulary from Part Two of the lecture. Work with a partner. Using the context and your knowledge of related words, take turns trying to guess the meanings of the words in **bold**.

_____ **1** During World War II, when thousands of men were fighting in Europe and Asia, women **took over** the men's jobs.

_____ **2** By the 1950s, more and more women were feeling **dissatisfied** with these roles.

_____ **3** Women working in business had almost no chance to become managers or **executives**.

_____ **4** [The book] was based on interviews with white, middle-class women living in the **suburbs**.

_____ **5** These women were very unhappy with their lives, with their **lack of** freedom and **lack of** a sense of identity.

_____ **6** [The book] became a huge **best seller**.

2 Work with your partner. Match the vocabulary terms with their definitions by writing the letter of each definition below in the blank next to the sentence or phrase containing the correct term in step 1. Check your answers in a dictionary if necessary.

    a not having something
    b begin to do something in place of another person who was doing it before
    c high-level worker with the power to make decisions
    d a new book that sells a large number of copies
    e areas outside the center of a city
    f not happy, not comfortable

⋒ NOTE TAKING: ORGANIZING YOUR NOTES IN A CHART

> Organizing your notes in a chart allows you to see the main ideas and supporting details of a lecture clearly. Charts are also useful for taking notes on comparisons.

1 Work with a partner. Study the following chart with notes from Part Two of the lecture. Discuss: How did the speaker organize the lecture? What information is missing from the notes? What do you think the abbreviations mean?

Pt 2: The _____

WW2	1950s	1960s	Today
♂: fighting in Europe, Asia	> ♀ started to feel dissat. w/ roles	1963: _____ _____ _____	Successes of WM: _____ _____ _____
♀: _____ _____ _____	– _____% worked	Book showed ____ _____	_____ _____
1945: _____ _____	– earned _____ of what ♂ earned for = job	_____ → beg. of _____ _____	_____ But: _____ _____
	– could be _____ _____	Mid 1960s: _____ _____ _____	_____ _____ _____
	– no ♀ _____	_____	Ineq. still exists

2 | Now listen to Part Two of the lecture and complete the notes. Use symbols and abbreviations. ▶ PLAY

3 | Work with a partner and compare your notes. Use them to retell the main events in the women's movement, decade by decade.

AFTER THE LECTURE

REVIEWING YOUR NOTES AFTER A LECTURE

Review your notes soon after a lecture in order to fill in information that you missed and to check that your notes are clear and correct. It is a good idea to work with a partner and ask each other questions, for example: What were the speaker's main points? What supporting details were provided? What did you learn? Finally, you should copy your notes neatly using any of the formats you have learned in this book.

1 | Work in two groups. Group A will prepare review questions on the civil rights movement, and Group B will prepare questions on the women's movement.

Example for Group A: *What was the civial rights movement?*

Example for Group B: *What did women do during World War II?*

Group A: The Civil Rights Movement	Group B: The Women's Movement
1 _____	1 _____
2 _____	2 _____
3 _____	3 _____
4 _____	4 _____
5 _____	5 _____
6 _____	6 _____
7 _____	7 _____

2 | Now work in small groups that each include people from Group A and Group B. Take turns asking and answering each other's questions about the lecture.

The Struggle Continues

Dr. Martin Luther King, Jr. (front row, seventh from right) led the March on Washington in 1963. He gave his famous "I Have a Dream" speech at the end of the march.

1 GETTING STARTED

In this section, you will read about progress toward equality in the United States from the 1960s until today. You will also hear several people talk about experiences in which they felt they received unfair treatment.

READING AND THINKING ABOUT THE TOPIC

1 │ Read the following passage.

In the 1960s, important laws were passed to protect the rights of African Americans, women, and immigrants. The passage of these laws encouraged other groups, such as Hispanics (also known as Latinos), older people (senior citizens), and people with disabilities to struggle for greater equality.

These groups have achieved some success in their struggles. For example, Latinos' protests have led to the introduction of ethnic studies programs at colleges across the country. New laws have guaranteed that older Americans have more access to public services, like transportation. And now, by law, public schools must provide assistance for children with disabilities.

However, the struggle for equality in the United States is not finished. Although laws have been passed to protect the rights of many groups, the laws are not always enforced or renewed. Furthermore, laws cannot change people's feelings. Despite the laws, *racism* (prejudice against people of different racial groups), *sexism* (prejudice against men or women because of their sex), *ageism* (prejudice against older people), and prejudice against people with disabilities still exist. The struggle for equality includes struggling to get rid of *stereotypes* (unfair, inaccurate generalizations) and promoting *tolerance* (acceptance) for all groups.

2 Answer the following questions according to the information in the passage:

1 What are some groups that have struggled for equality since the 1960s?
2 What were some of the achievements of these groups?
3 Why is it necessary to continue the struggle for equality today?

3 Read these questions and share your responses with a partner:

1 What are some examples of stereotypes? Why are stereotypes unfair?
2 What are some examples of equality or inequality in other countries you know about?

⌢ LISTENING FOR SPECIFIC INFORMATION

1 You will hear four people describe situations in which they believe they were treated unfairly. Read the summaries below before listening and predict the type of information you need to listen for.

1	3
Peter is _____ years old. _____ months ago, he lost his job as a _____ because the company didn't have _____ for him. But then the company hired a new _____ who is _____ years old.	Robert is married and has _____ children. Last week, he and his wife filled out an application for a new _____. However, they didn't get it. A friend told them it's because nobody else in the building has _____, and the manager is worried about _____.
2	**4**
Theresa is a _____. Last week she had an _____ for a job with a _____. It went well until _____, when the interviewer asked her if she was pregnant. She said _____. She didn't get the job.	Rebecca is a _____ who uses a _____. One of her classes is on the _____ floor and the building has only two _____, so she has been _____ to class a few times. She explained the problem to her professor, but he expects her to come to class _____ just like everyone else.

2 Now listen to the four people and fill in the missing information. **▶ PLAY**

3 Compare answers in small groups. Then, for each situation, discuss the following question: Do you believe the speaker was treated fairly or unfairly? Why or why not?

In this section, you will hear an interview with Robin, who works with the blind (people who cannot see). Then you will hear Jairo and Sandy discuss progress toward equality for Latinos and senior citizens.

BEFORE THE INTERVIEWS

BUILDING BACKGROUND KNOWLEDGE

1 How much do you know about people with disabilities, Latinos, and senior citizens – three groups who are still struggling for greater equality in the United States? Work with a partner. Read the facts below, which are based on the United States census of 2000, and guess which number from the box matches each item. Write the number in the blank next to the item.

2	47
12	52
19	54
28	76
30	

1 Number of Latino senators _____

2 Percentage of the U.S. population over age 65 _____

3 Millions of Americans with a disability _____

4 Percentage of Latinos who complete high school _____

5 Average life expectancy for men and women _____

6 Percentage of disabled people who are unemployed _____

7 Percentage of Latinos who are homeowners _____

8 Percentage of men age 65+ in the workforce _____

9 Percentage of disabled people who live in poverty _____

2 With your partner, look at the correct answers at the bottom of this page. Then discuss the numbers that were higher or lower than your guesses.

Answers to step 1:
1 2; 2 12; 3 54; 4 52; 5 76; 6 30; 7 47; 8 19; 9 28

INTERVIEW WITH ROBIN: Working with the blind

Here are some words and phrases from the interview with Robin printed in **bold** and given in the context in which you will hear them. They are followed by definitions.

There are computers that can "talk," and software that prints documents in **Braille**: *a system of printing that allows blind people to read by touching with their fingers*

There are many simple **gadgets** . . . that can help: *small machines*

A tray . . . is one of the simplest **aids**: *things that help*

By folding a **bill** a certain way . . . : *paper money, such as $1 or $5*

You leave **singles** flat: *one-dollar bills ($1)*

Their problems are **overwhelming**: *very great or large*

They learn how to do things **on their own**: *without help from others*

Robin

🎧 LISTENING FOR SPECIFIC INFORMATION

1 | Robin works with blind people. In the interview, she talks about ways that blind people can live and work more independently. Look at the pictures below and discuss this question with a partner: How do you think the items in the pictures can help blind people?

a _____   b _____   c _____

d _____   e _____

2 | Now listen to the interview. Write the names of the items in the blanks. ▶ **PLAY**

3 | Work with a partner and compare your answers. Discuss how these items make life easier for the blind.

INTERVIEW WITH JAIRO and SANDY: The struggle of two groups for equality

Here are some words and phrases from the interview printed in **bold** and given in the context in which you will hear them. They are followed by definitions.

Latinos have made important **contributions** to American society: *something people do or give in order to make something better or more successful*

[Latinos] are the largest **minority group** in the United States: *a group of people from a particular racial, ethnic, or religious background other than the white majority*

When patients come in, there are **interpreters**: *people who translate from one language to another*

Patients don't have to struggle to explain their **symptoms** in English: *evidence of medical problems*

There's still a lot of **poverty** in the Hispanic community: *being poor*

There are laws, but they're really hard to **enforce**: *make people obey*

A lot of times, the boss thinks **there's a risk**: *it's dangerous*

. . . if he's got two **applicants** for a job: *people trying to get a job*

Jairo

Sandy

🎧 LISTENING FOR MAIN IDEAS

1 | Look at the chart below and notice the kind of information you need to listen for. Make a larger chart on your own paper.

	Group	Progress toward equality	Problems that still exist
Jairo			
Sandy			

2 | Now listen to the interviews. Take notes in your chart. ▶ **PLAY**

3 | Work with a partner and compare answers. Then choose a group in the United States or another country that you would like to discuss. Add a row to your chart and make notes on your group. Discuss your ideas with your partner.

AFTER THE INTERVIEWS

SHARING YOUR OPINION

1 Having tolerance for other people means accepting people who are different without prejudice. *Mix It Up*, a program designed to teach tolerance, asks students in schools and colleges to write about their experiences with intolerance. Students across the country contribute poems and essays to the program's Web site.

Read "Walls: A Poem for Tolerance," the poem in the left column below. It was written by Pebbles Salas, a student in the eighth grade.

2 Work with a partner and answer the questions in the right column.

Walls:
A Poem for Tolerance

People make **boundaries**
they classify who's who.
Even if they don't know you,
they classify you too.
Whether it's color or style,
they'll **file you down**
to which groups you can be with,
and which groups you can't **hang around**.
People don't see the good and the bad,
they just imagine your face,
would it look good on an **ad**?
People are sad when they **get rejected**
they sit with a different group
to feel protected.
But social boundaries can be **such a drag**,
you **wrap up** new friendships in one little bag.
Would you want one pair of friends,
or would you care for two?
That decision is **solely** up to you.
So if you sit at the same table every day,
there will be no new friendships,
only old friendships will stay.

Questions

1 What do most people do, in Pebbles' opinion? What consequence does this have?

2 What do people imagine, according to Pebbles? Why is this bad, in her opinion?

3 How do people feel when they are not accepted? What do they do, and why?

4 What are social boundaries? What does Pebbles think of them?

5 What should people do if they want to have more friends?

boundaries: limits
file you down: limit you
hang around: be with
ad: advertisement
get rejected: not accepted
such a drag: really bad
wrap up: put
solely: only

3 Work in small groups and discuss the following questions:

  1 What is the meaning of the word *Walls* in the title of the poem?

  2 What is the main point that Pebbles is making?

  3 How might this poem be different if it were about adults or people in their late teens?

  4 If Jairo and Sandy read this poem, what do you think they would say?

  5 Do you think poetry can be helpful in making people aware of the importance of being tolerant? Do you think this poem is helpful? Why or why not?

4 Look at the photograph below. In your group, discuss this question: How does this photograph relate to the ideas in "Walls"?

In this section, you will participate in an activity that explores stereotypes, tolerance, and discrimination. Then you will give a group presentation about what you learned.

THINKING CRITICALLY ABOUT THE TOPIC

You will not always agree with what you read or hear. Make it a habit to evaluate what other people say and compare it to your own knowledge and experiences.

1 | Work in small groups. Read the descriptions of the three activities below and choose one that your group would like to do.

1 Examine gender roles
Make a two-column chart, one column headed "Men" and the other column headed "Women." Then choose a popular magazine and count the number of men and women in the advertisements. Put this information next to the headings in the appropriate column. Underneath, list the roles that the men and women are playing, for example, husband, wife, teacher, athlete, businessperson, and so on. Analyze the results of your research. Are there more women or more men in the ads? What roles do they play? Are these stereotypical roles, or do they show men and women in a realistic way?

2 Analyze a quotation about tolerance

Choose two or three of the quotations below or find others by doing an Internet search for "tolerance quotations" or "quotations about tolerance." Discuss the meaning of the quotations and give examples from your experience that show why you agree or disagree with them.

- *You must look into people, as well as at them.*
  Lord Chesterfield (1694–1773), British statesman

- *Sometimes I feel discriminated against, but it does not make me angry. It merely astonishes me. How can any deny themselves the pleasure of my company?*
  Zora Neale Hurston (1891–1960), American novelist

- *People are very open-minded about new things – as long as they're exactly like the old ones.*
  Charles F. Kettering (1876–1958), American inventor

- *Darkness cannot drive out darkness; only light can do that. Hate cannot drive out hate; only love can do that.*
  Dr. Martin Luther King, Jr. (1929–1968), American civil rights leader

- *The only way to make sure people you agree with can speak is to support the rights of people you don't agree with.*
  Eleanor Holmes Norton (1937–), member of U.S. House of Representatives

- *Those wearing tolerance for a label*
  Call other views intolerable
  Phyllis McGinley (1905–1978), American poet

3 Share an experience of discrimination

Tell the members of your group about a time when someone or some group discriminated against you because of your academic ability, athletic ability, hobbies/interests, gender, personal appearance, family income, home environment, or other factor. Explain how you felt and why you think you were the victim of discrimination. Listen to your classmates' stories. Discuss the similarities and differences between their experiences and yours.

2 When you have finished your activity, discuss the following questions with the members of your group:

1 What did you learn from doing this activity?

2 What was the most interesting part?

GIVING AN ORAL PRESENTATION

Prepare a group presentation about your activity to give to the class. Describe what you did and summarize the results of your discussions. Make sure everyone in the group participates in the presentation.

4 ACADEMIC LISTENING AND NOTE TAKING: Two Important Laws in the Struggle for Equality

In this section, you will hear and take notes on a two-part lecture by David Chachere, a lecturer on sociology. The title of his lecture is *Two Important Laws in the Struggle for Equality*. Mr. Chachere will talk about the Age Discrimination in Employment Act of 1967 and the Americans with Disabilities Act of 1990.

BEFORE THE LECTURE

SHARING YOUR OPINION

Look at the photographs below and discuss the following questions with a partner:

1 What do the people in the photographs have in common?
2 What difficulties do these people probably face?
3 How could laws help these people to participate fully in society?

Woodworker

Student

Athlete

Office worker

⌕ NOTE TAKING: LISTENING FOR SIGNAL WORDS AND PHRASES

Good lecturers use *signal words and phrases* to help listeners follow the organization of their lectures and to understand the relationship between ideas. Signal words and phrases have many different purposes. For example:

Purpose	Signal words and phrases
To add an idea	*also / as well as / in addition*
To emphasize	*of course / in fact*
To indicate difference	*however / in contrast / on the other hand*
To indicate similarity	*(just) like / similar to*
To indicate time	*before / after / while / during*
To introduce a cause or reason	*because / since*
To introduce an effect	*as a result / therefore / consequently*
To introduce a topic or change of topic	*as for / speaking of*
To list information or ideas	*first / second / next / last / to begin*
To refer to information mentioned earlier	*to refresh your memory / remember / as I said*
To repeat an idea with different words	*in other words / that is*
To show order of importance	*more / the most important*
To signal an incomplete list	*etcetera / and so forth / and so on*

1 Work with a partner. Read the following sentences from the lecture and try to predict which signal words or phrases from the box go in the blanks.

1 _____ . . . the '60s was an important decade because during this time several important laws gave more rights to women, African Americans, and immigrants.

2 Let's begin with the first one, the Age Discrimination Act. I think we need to talk about, _____, the reasons why this law was needed, second, what it does, and _____, well, its impact.

3 _____ this law, employers could set an age limit for job applicants.

4 Well, of course it [the law] refers to hiring and firing. _____, age can't be used as a reason for refusing to hire an older person.

5 _____, age can't be used as a reason to promote someone to a better position.

6 The ADA _____ covers people who face discrimination _____ they have a serious illness like cancer.

7 And _____ non-physical disabilities, did you know that some businesses are starting to hire some people with mental disabilities if they are capable of doing a particular job?

8 But I think _____ impact of this law is that it has helped to change the way we think.

9 In many places in the world, people with disabilities have to stay at home _____ there is no way for them to get around.

2 | Listen and fill in the blanks with the signal words or phrases you hear. ▶ **PLAY**

3 | Work with your partner and compare answers. Then select other signal words and phrases from the box that are appropriate for the blanks.

LECTURE, PART ONE: The Age Discrimination in Employment Act

GUESSING VOCABULARY FROM CONTEXT

1 | The following items contain important vocabulary from Part One of the lecture. Work with a partner. Using the context and your knowledge of related words, take turns trying to guess the meanings of the words in **bold**.

_____ **1** I think we need to talk about, first, the reasons why this law was needed, second, what it does, and third, its **impact**.

_____ **2** Before this law, employers could **set** an age limit for job applicants.

_____ **3** In addition, age can't be used as a reason to **promote** someone to a better position.

_____ **4** Older workers can get the same **benefits** as younger people.

_____ **5** **Mandatory** retirement is not allowed nowadays.

_____ **6** Your company cannot force you to **retire**.

_____ **7** There are still many thousands of legal **complaints** about age discrimination each year.

_____ **8** Companies are **more than 40 percent more likely** to interview a younger job applicant than an older job applicant.

2 | Work with your partner. Match the vocabulary terms with their definitions by writing the letter of each definition below in the blank next to the sentence or phrase containing the correct term in step 1. Check your answers in a dictionary if necessary.

    a stop working because of your age
    b effect, result
    c move a person up to a higher level in a job
    d make, establish
    e required, forced, something you must do
    f advantages people get from their employers besides their salaries, such as health insurance
    g when someone says something is wrong or not satisfactory
    h the possibility is at least 40 percent higher

🎧 NOTE TAKING: INDENTING

Indenting can help you to see the difference between main ideas and supporting details. You can use indenting with other note-taking techniques, such as bullets, numbers, or letters. Continue to indent as the information becomes more specific. For example:

1. Main idea (not indented)
- **First supporting detail** (indented 5 spaces from the left margin)
  - **More specific information about the detail** (indented 10 spaces)
- **Second supporting detail** (indented 5 spaces)

1 These are a student's notes on Part One of the lecture. But it is hard to follow them because the student didn't separate main ideas from supporting details. Read the notes and try to predict which items are main ideas and which ones are details.

> Age Discrim. in Employment Act
>
> Why law was needed
> Older people faced discrim. in wkplace:
> Before law, employers could set age limits, e.g., 35
>
> What the law does
> Protects people > 40 from discrim.
> Can't use age to:
> refuse to hire
> fire
> promote to a better position
>
> Impact of law
> nowadays, nothing about age in job app
> equal benefits for older + younger people
> no mandatory retirement
> Do employers follow law?
> 1000s of complaints per year → age discrim. still exists
> Recent study showed companies 40% more likely to interview younger applicant
> But: People are more aware of age discrim. than before law

2 Listen to Part One of the lecture. Mark the main ideas and supporting details by writing numbers, bullets, or other symbols you prefer in the margin. ▶ **PLAY**

3 Rewrite the notes on your own paper with the symbols you chose in step 2. Be sure to indent them appropriately.

4 Work in small groups and compare your notes. Use them to retell the information in Part One of the lecture.

LECTURE, PART TWO: The Americans with Disabilities Act

GUESSING VOCABULARY FROM CONTEXT

1 | The following items contain important vocabulary from Part Two of the lecture. Work with a partner. Using the context and your knowledge of related words, take turns trying to guess the meanings of the words in **bold**.

_____ **1** The Americans with Disabilities Act . . . is often called the ADA **for short**.

_____ **2** By _disability_ we mean . . . any physical or **mental condition** that limits a person's ability to participate in a major life activity.

_____ **3** If you've ridden a public bus in an American city, . . . you know that they all have special **mechanisms** . . .

_____ **4** In many places in the world, . . . there is no way for [people with disabilities] to **get around**.

_____ **5** They are also often **rejected** by society.

_____ **6** Let the **shameful** wall of exclusion finally come tumbling down.

_____ **7** What this means is that our goal needs to be **inclusion**.

2 | Work with your partner. Match the vocabulary terms with their definitions by writing the letter of each definition below in the blank next to the sentence or phrase containing the correct term in step 1. Check your answers in a dictionary if necessary.

a causing great embarrassment
b technology, gadgets
c a sickness of the mind that affects people's behavior and emotions
d as an abbreviation
e move from place to place
f including everybody, accepting everybody
g unwanted, not accepted

⌒ NOTE TAKING: USING AN OUTLINE

Using an outline is a traditional way to organize notes in English-speaking countries. In a formal outline, main ideas are usually listed using roman numerals (I, II, III, etc.). Subdivisions of main ideas are indicated as capital letters (A, B, C, etc.). Supporting details are listed using Arabic numerals (1, 2, 3, etc.). Each level of detail is indented under the level above it.

You may not be able to organize your notes carefully while you are actually listening to a lecture. In that case, you should rewrite your notes as soon as possible after the lecture and put them into an appropriate, well-organized format.

1 Look at the outlined notes for the beginning of Part Two of the lecture below. Work with a partner and discuss the following questions:

    1 What is the main idea of this section of Part Two?

    2 What are the subdivisions of the main idea?

    3 Which examples are given?

> The Americans with Disabilities Act (ADA)
>
> I. ADA
>   A. Passed in 1990
>   B. Protects ppl w/ disabil. in diff places, e.g.,
>   1. work
>   2. housing
>   3. educ.

2 Look at a student's notes for the rest of the lecture. They are not in outline form. Read the notes and try to predict which items are main ideas, which ones are subdivisions of main ideas, and which ones are supporting details.

> Def of "disability"
> Physical
> Mental
>
> Impact of ADA
> Changed life for disabled people, e.g.,
> buses have mechanisms to help ppl in wheelchairs
> doorways must be wide
> some businesses hiring ppl w/ nonphysical (mental) disab
> Sts w/ learning disab can get more time on tests
>
> Most important impact of law: Change ppl's thinking
> Some countries: Disabled stay home b/c no way to get around
> U.S.: Understand there are many things disabled ppl can do
> Pres. Bush (1990) said: "Let the shameful wall of exclusion finally come
>   tumbling down."
> Goal must be inclusion

3 Listen to Part Two of the lecture. Put the notes above into an outline by writing roman numerals, capital letters, and numbers in the margin in appropriate places.
   ▶ PLAY

4 Rewrite the notes in outline form on your own paper.

5 Work in small groups and compare your notes. Use them to retell the information in Part Two.

AFTER THE LECTURE

USING YOUR NOTES TO MAKE A TIME LINE

When you are studying a topic in which events and their dates are important, it is useful to make a time line from the information in your notes. This helps you review what you have learned in a visual way.

1 | Work with a partner. Use the information from Chapters 5 and 6 to construct a time line of important steps the United States has taken toward equality. You can either make a time line on your own paper or add lines to the incomplete time line below.

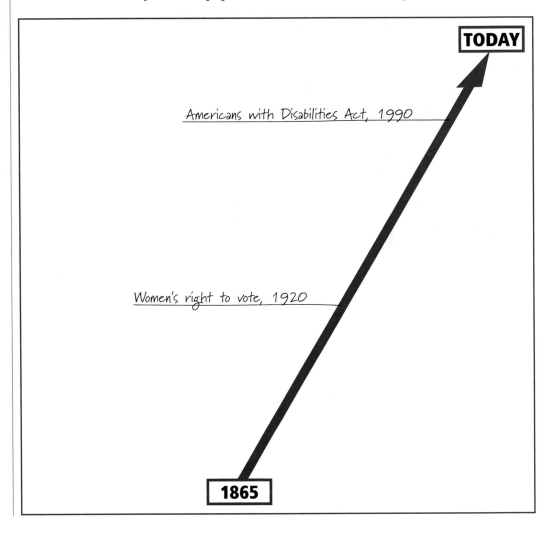

TODAY

Americans with Disabilities Act, 1990

Women's right to vote, 1920

1865

2 | As you work, discuss the following question: What are the causes and the effects of each event in your time line?

3 | As a class, compare the information in your time lines. Make a class time line on the board.

American Values

4TH JULY PARADE, N.Y. 7/4/11

Since 1776, Independence Day (Fourth of July) celebrations have been an important part of American culture.

In this unit, you will consider some of the values that defined the United States in the past and that still play an important role in people's lives today. Chapter 7 focuses on some of the traditional values that form the foundation of American culture and society. You will hear interviews with people about values that are important to them. The lecture in this chapter focuses on three American folk heroes and the values they represent. Chapter 8 concerns ways in which traditional values have changed in modern America. You will hear young people talking about differences between their values and those of their parents and a teacher talking about values that are important for students to learn. The lecture in this chapter is about conservative and liberal political views in America.

Chapter **7**

American Values from the Past

① GETTING STARTED

In this section, you will learn about some traditional values that many Americans hold.

READING AND THINKING ABOUT THE TOPIC

1 | Read the following passage.

Values are beliefs that help us decide what is right and wrong and how we should behave in various situations. They guide our personal, social, and business behavior and affect every aspect of our daily lives.

Many Western values are based on beliefs that originally came from both the ancient Greek and Roman civilizations and the religious beliefs of Judaism and Christianity. American values are also based on these beliefs. However, the beliefs of the Protestant branch of Christianity have been particularly important in American culture because many of America's early settlers and leaders came from a Protestant tradition that emphasizes hard work. Sometimes, therefore, the value of hard work is referred to as "the Protestant work ethic." Traditional American values include hard work, self-reliance, equality, freedom, individualism, and democracy. All of these values have defined American culture since the earliest days of the nation's history.

2 Answer the following questions according to the information in the passage:

1 What are values, and what is their purpose?

2 Which cultures and religions have influenced American values?

3 What are some key American values?

3 Read these questions and share your responses with a partner:

1 Do you think that most values are the same from culture to culture?

2 What are three or four values that you believe in?

🎧 LISTENING FOR SPECIFIC INFORMATION

1 Read the following paragraph.

> Horatio Alger was a famous nineteenth-century American author. He wrote more than 130 best-selling stories about poor boys who achieved the American dream of success because they were hardworking, honest, kind, brave, and determined. The moral messages in these books encouraged Americans to believe in "the American dream" – the idea that hard work would lead to success even for people who were poor and who did not have the support of their families.

2 Read this summary of a Horatio Alger story written in 1877. Then listen and underline the details you hear. ▶ **PLAY**

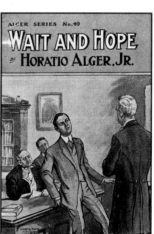

The title of this story is *Wait and Hope,* and it is about a boy called [**1** Steve/Ben], whose parents [**2** have died/are very poor]. The boy [**3** has a lot of friends who help him/ has few friends, but he refuses to lose hope]. He feels very [**4** sad/positive] about his life. One day, he meets a [**5** rich stranger/a lost relative], who gives him a job. He works hard at school and finally manages to begin studying at [**6** Princeton University/Harvard University]. His story shows that if you have [**7** patience and strength/good luck and determination], you will eventually find success.

3 Share your reactions to this story with your classmates. Discuss these questions:

1 Which values are illustrated by this story?

2 Are these values important to you?

3 Why do you think this kind of story has always been so popular in America?

2 AMERICAN VOICES: Marielena, Dan, Anne-Marie, and Leila

In this section, you will hear four Americans talk about values that are important to them as well as values that sometimes create disagreement.

BEFORE THE INTERVIEWS

BUILDING VOCABULARY

L. Robert Kohls was a writer and teacher in the field of intercultural studies. In a famous paper called "The Values Americans Live By," written in the 1980s, Dr. Kohls described 13 basic values that help explain why Americans feel and act as they do.

1 Read Kohls's list of values on the left and match them with the examples on the right. Write the letters of the examples in the blanks.

		Value	Example
c	1	Action and work	**a** "Try a new hair color today!" (advertisement)
	2	Change (Change is positive.)	**b** "This car gets better mileage than any other car on the market." (comment from one friend to another)
	3	Competition	**c** "Don't just stand there: Do something!" (popular saying)
	4	Directness / Honesty	**d** "Why be number two, when you can be number one?" (comment from one salesperson to another)
	5	Efficiency	**e** "Tomorrow, tomorrow, I love you, tomorrow, you're always a day away." (Line from the Broadway show *Annie*)
	6	Equality	**f** "Never tell lies." (lesson to children)
	7	Future orientation (The future is better than the past.)	**g** All men are created equal. (from the Declaration of Independence)
	8	Individualism	**h** "You have the power to change your life." (advice from one friend to another)

	Value	Example
_____ 9	Informality	**i** Save time, keep time, use time, be on time, spend time, waste time, lose time, gain time, kill time (English idioms)
_____ 10	Materialism	**j** "That's what we call success!" (advertisement for a big car)
_____ 11	Personal control and responsibility for one's life / Independence	**k** There's no one on earth exactly like you. (common belief)
_____ 12	Self-reliance	**l** "Just call me Joe." (teacher's request to students)
_____ 13	Time	**m** More than 100 words begin with the prefix *self-*. (fact)

2 Work in small groups and compare answers. Then discuss these questions:

1 From your experience, do you agree that these values are important to Americans?

2 Which of these values are important to you? Give examples.

3 What are some other values that you think are important to Americans?

INTERVIEW WITH MARIELENA AND DAN: Personal values

Here are some words and phrases from the interview printed in **bold** and given in the context in which you will hear them. They are followed by definitions.

I want her to realize that she has a lot of **options**: *possibilities, choices*

The **expectation** in my family is that the children will become professionals: *goal, hope*

There are many ways to be happy and **productive**: *useful, creative*

I want [my daughter] to find a career that is **suitable** . . . for her: *appropriate*

I think maybe she'll become . . . a **chef**!: *a person whose job is cooking in a restaurant*

The first [value] I think of is hard work. And **self-reliance**: *depending on yourself*

It's important to work toward goals that you **set** for yourself: *choose*

Marielena

Dan

🎧 ANSWERING TRUE/FALSE/NOT SURE QUESTIONS

When answering true/false questions, you are sometimes given three options: *T* (true), *F* (false), or *NI* (not enough information). You should respond *NI* if the speaker does not provide enough details for you to decide if a statement is true or false.

1 Read the following statements before you listen to the interview with Marielena and Dan.

Marielena

_____ **1** The value that Marielena considers most important is education.

_____ **2** Marielena has a daughter and a son.

_____ **3** Her daughter is 15.

_____ **4** There are many artists in Marielena's family.

_____ **5** She thinks her daughter might become a painter or an actress.

Dan

_____ **1** The value Dan considers most important is competition.

_____ **2** Dan is 20 years old.

_____ **3** He thinks it is important to improve yourself.

_____ **4** Dan wants to go to graduate school.

_____ **5** His part-time job is in a restaurant.

2 Now listen to the interviews. Write *T* (true), *F* (false), or *NI* (not enough information) next to each of the statements. ▶ **PLAY**

3 Work with a partner and compare your answers to step 2. Then discuss this question: Do you agree with Marielena and Dan's values?

INTERVIEW WITH ANNE-MARIE AND LEILA: Disagreeing with traditional values

Here are some words and phrases from the interview with Anne-Marie and Leila printed in **bold** and given in the context in which you will hear them. They are followed by definitions.

It's a matter of respect: *It's something people do to show respect*

People **treat each other on a first-name basis**: *call each other by their first names*

Now that is **way** too informal: *much*

People are more **tactful**!: *careful not to say anything that will upset or embarrass other people*

You don't want to be **greedy**, so you say, "No, thanks.": *always wanting more*

I think we're too direct. It's **rude**: *not polite*

He went straight for the refrigerator and **helped himself to** some juice: *took, gave himself*

Anne-Marie

Leila

🎧 LISTENING FOR MAIN IDEAS

1 | Read the statements below.

1 Americans are

_____ **a** too direct.

_____ **b** too informal.

2 They

_____ **a** accept food immediately if it is offered.

_____ **b** ask to look around your house.

_____ **c** call each other by their first names.

_____ **d** state their opinion too directly.

_____ **e** wear jeans everywhere they go.

2 | Now listen to the interviews. Identify which speaker, Anne-Marie or Leila, makes each of the comments above. Write *A-M* or *L* on the lines. ▶ **PLAY**

3 | Compare answers with a partner. Go over each of the statements and say whether you agree or disagree.

AFTER THE INTERVIEWS

SHARING YOUR OPINION

1 | Read the situations below and circle the letter, *a* or *b*, that comes closest to your reaction.

1 Your neighbor says: "My daughter's going to drop her physics class and take music instead. She says physics is too hard. I'm worried she won't be able to get into a top university."

You think:
a I agree with the daughter. Why should she take a subject she's not interested in?
b The daughter should just work harder at physics. She needs to think about her future.

2 Your 20-year-old friend says: "I'm going to work at a bookstore and keep going to school full-time."

You say:
a "That's a bad idea. Your grades will probably go down, and you'll be too tired to spend time with friends."
b "That's a good idea. You'll learn how to be responsible and manage your time better."

3 Your 45-year-old father says: "I've decided I don't really like my job. I want to go back to school and change careers."

You say:
a "I don't think you should do that. You're too old to go back to school."
b "That's great. You've worked hard for 20 years, and now you deserve the chance to do a job you really enjoy."

4 Your professor comes to class wearing jeans.

You think:
a I feel comfortable with a teacher who dresses informally.
b I can't respect a teacher who dresses like a student.

5 At the bank, the bank teller calls you by your first name.

You think:
a That's disrespectful.
b I like the casual, friendly atmosphere of this bank.

2 | Work with a partner and compare your answers. Which values explain your point of view in each case?

3 IN YOUR OWN VOICE

In this section, you will read some common sayings in English and discuss the values that they represent. Then you will make a presentation about one of the sayings and respond to your classmates' presentations.

GIVING AN ORAL PRESENTATION

1 | Work with a partner. Read the list of sayings below and look up any words you do not know in a dictionary. Then write an explanation of each item.

1 A penny saved is a penny earned.

_____

2 Always stand on your own two feet.

_____

3 In trying times (difficult times), don't stop trying.

_____

4 Punctuality is the key to success.

_____

5 When life gives you lemons, make lemonade.

_____

6 When you make your bed, you must lie in it.

_____

7 Tomorrow is another day.

_____

8 Some people have tact; others tell the truth.

_____

9 Men are born equal, but they are also born different.

_____

10 Efficiency is doing better what is already being done.

_____

2 | With your partner, prepare a short (2–4 minute) presentation on one of the sayings that you agree or disagree with.

- Explain what the saying means in your own words.
- Say which value(s) the saying suggests.
- Say why you agree or disagree with the saying.
- Tell a story or give an example from your experience that illustrates the saying.

3 | Listen to your classmates' presentations and take notes. Then use your notes to make comments or ask questions about anything you did not understand.

4 ACADEMIC LISTENING AND NOTE TAKING: Three American Folk Heroes

In this section, you will hear and take notes on a two-part lecture by Peter Roman, a professor of political science. The title of his lecture is *Three American Folk Heroes*. A *folk hero* is a real or imaginary figure who does extraordinary things or has extraordinary powers that help people. Professor Roman explains how these heroes represent many important American values. In the second part of the lecture, he answers questions from students.

BEFORE THE LECTURE

SHARING YOUR KNOWLEDGE

The pictures below show three types of American folk heroes. Work in small groups. Look at each picture and discuss the following questions:

1 What adjectives can you use to describe this person or character?

2 What values does this person or character represent?

3 Why do many Americans think of this kind of person or character as a hero?

Bill Gates

Cowboy

Superman

🎧 NOTE TAKING: LISTENING FOR KEY WORDS

> *Key words* are the words and expressions that tell you which topic a speaker is discussing. You can recognize these important terms in several ways:
>
> Key words are often repeated: *Let's begin with the **cowboy**. Think about all the places you see **cowboys**. If you turn on the TV, I guarantee you'll find a **cowboy** movie on one of the channels! And the image of the **cowboy** is also seen constantly in advertising and fashion.*
>
> Key words are often stressed: *Let's begin with the COWBOY.*

1 Listen to some parts of the lecture that include key words. As you listen, fill in the blanks with the key words you hear. ▶ **PLAY**

1 This afternoon, I'm going to talk about three traditional American _____. And by _____ I mean real people or imaginary figures who do extraordinary things or who have extraordinary powers.

2 Let's begin with the _____. Think about all the places you see _____. If you turn on the TV, I guarantee you'll find a _____ movie on one of the channels! And the image of the _____ is also seen constantly in advertising and fashion.

3 An _____ is a person who starts a company, who makes business deals in order to make a profit. We think of _____ as people who have great ideas and take risks. And the _____ is also a very powerful symbol of American values.

4 There are all kinds of _____ – Superman, Batman, Spider-Man, and so on. And _____ – well, if you can't save yourself, they will!

2 Work with a partner and compare answers.

3 With your partner, take turns reading the items in step 1 out loud. Make sure to stress the underlined words.

LECTURE, PART ONE: *Three American Folk Heroes*

GUESSING VOCABULARY FROM CONTEXT

1 The following items contain important vocabulary from Part One of the lecture. Work with a partner. Using the context and your knowledge of related words, take turns trying to guess the meanings of the words in **bold**.

_____ **1** Folk heroes . . . do **extraordinary** things or . . . have **extraordinary** powers.

_____ **2** People began moving West in order to **make their fortune**.

_____ **3** Some of these settlers started large **cattle ranches**.

_____ **4** [The cowboy] is completely **self-reliant**.

_____ **5** We think of entrepreneurs as people who have great ideas and **take risks**.

_____ **6** The last American hero I'd like you to think about is **imaginary**.

_____ **7** Most Americans **relate** very strongly **to** the values that the superhero represents.

2 Work with your partner. Match the vocabulary terms with their definitions by writing the letter of each definition below in the blank next to the sentence or phrase containing the correct term in step 1. Check your answers in a dictionary if necessary.

a very unusual and special
b feel strongly connected with
c do something where there is the possibility of danger or failure
d depending only on yourself
e not real
f large areas of land where people raise animals for food
g become rich and successful

🎧 NOTE TAKING: CLARIFYING YOUR NOTES

You may find that there are parts of a lecture that you cannot understand because the speaker is talking too quickly. This often happens during a lecture, so do not panic! As you are taking notes, develop a system for marking ideas or words that you need to check. For example, you can use circles, question marks, or asterisks to mark parts that you do not understand. You can also write short questions to yourself or insert a blank line when you have missed an important point.

If possible, clarify any information that you do not understand during the lecture. Most lecturers will encourage you to ask questions. After the lecture, review your notes and ask the lecturer or a classmate about anything that still is not clear.

1 Look at a student's notes on the beginning of Professor Roman's lecture. The circles, question marks, and asterisks indicate things that the student did not understand.

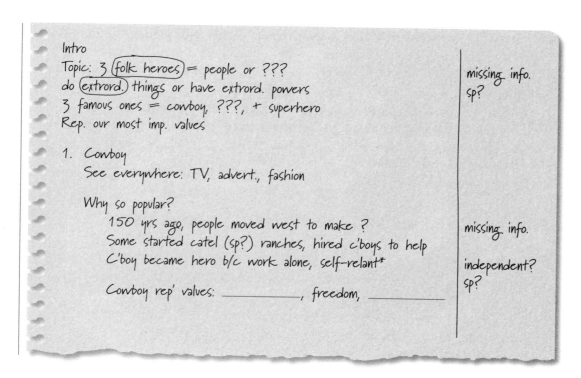

Intro
Topic: 3 (folk heroes) = people or ???   missing info.
do (extrord.) things or have extrord. powers   sp?
3 famous ones = cowboy, ???, + superhero
Rep. our most imp. values

1. Cowboy
    See everywhere: TV, advert., fashion

    Why so popular?
        150 yrs ago, people moved west to make ?   missing info.
        Some started catel (sp?) ranches, hired c'boys to help
        C'boy became hero b/c work alone, self-relant*   independent?
                                                          sp?
    Cowboy rep' values: _____, freedom, _____

2 Copy the notes above onto your own paper. Then listen to Part One of the lecture. Listen for the information missing from the student's notes and fill it in. Then continue taking notes on the rest of Part One. Use circles, question marks, asterisks, blank spaces, and questions to mark parts of the lecture you did not understand.
▶ PLAY

3 Work in small groups. Review and clarify your notes by asking your classmates questions about the parts you marked. Listen to the lecture again if necessary.

4 Copy your notes neatly, using any format you prefer.

LECTURE, PART TWO: Questions and Answers

GUESSING VOCABULARY FROM CONTEXT

1 The following items contain important vocabulary from Part Two of the lecture. Work with a partner. Using the context and your knowledge of related words, take turns trying to guess the meanings of the words in **bold**.

_____ **1** [The time] after the Civil War . . . was a period of huge industrial **expansion**.

_____ **2** Andrew Carnegie . . . made millions of dollars from his steel **factories**.

_____ **3** The first Superman **comic book** was written . . . in the 1930s.

_____ **4** [*The Incredibles*] was one of the most **profitable** movies in history!

_____ **5** She gave [a lot of money] to different **charities**.

2 Work with your partner. Match the vocabulary terms with their definitions by writing the letter of each definition below in the blank next to the sentence or phrase containing the correct term in step 1. Check your answers in a dictionary if necessary.

    a organizations that give money or help to people who need it
    b buildings where people use machines to make products
    c a magazine that uses drawings to tell stories
    d growth, becoming larger
    e making a lot of money

⌒ NOTE TAKING: TAKING NOTES ON QUESTIONS AND ANSWERS

It is common for lecturers to ask students if they have any questions or comments. At this time, you can ask the lecturer to explain ideas that you did not understand, request additional information, or make a comment.

Pay attention when your classmates ask questions and listen carefully to the lecturer's answers. Take notes on new information you hear.

1 Read the following questions from Part Two of the lecture. Work with a partner and try to predict Professor Roman's answers.

    1 Could you explain a little more about entrepreneurs?
    2 Did Superman also exist in the nineteenth century?
    3 Why didn't you talk about any women folk heroes?

2 Listen to Part Two of the lecture. As you listen, take notes on the lecturer's responses to the questions. ▶ PLAY

3 Work with a partner and clarify your notes as needed. Then rewrite them neatly and add them to your notes from Part One.

The Incredibles

Annie Oakley

AFTER THE LECTURE

SHARING YOUR OPINION

1 | Read the following true stories. Take notes on the values that you think the people in these stories have. You may list values from this chapter or other values that you think are appropriate.

1 Victoria Ruvolo, a 44-year-old woman, was driving on a highway when some teenagers threw a frozen turkey at her car. She suffered very bad injuries. When she recovered and met her 18-year-old attacker in court, she hugged him. She told him to do good things with his life and persuaded the judge not to send him to prison for 25 years.

2 Police officer Rocco Marini learned that a pregnant woman was about to have a baby. He ran out of the office, drove to her home, and delivered a healthy baby boy in her living room. He said it was a really nice feeling to be able to help the new mother.

3 Haider Sediqi, a cab driver in Los Angeles, found $350,000 worth of jewelry in his taxicab. He returned the jewels to the owner, who rewarded him by sending him a check for $10,000 and a diamond bracelet.

4 Aron Ralston was hiking in the mountains when he was trapped by a huge rock that fell on his arm. After six days, he cut off the lower part of his own arm to save his life. He says that this was the most beautiful experience he will ever have because it gave him the gift of life.

5 Wesley Autry, a 50-year-old construction worker, was waiting for the New York subway with his two young daughters when a man nearby collapsed and fell onto the tracks in the path of an approaching train. Autry told his girls to stay where they were, jumped down onto the tracks and held the man flat on the ground, covering him with his body. The train rolled over them, one-half inch above their heads. Both men escaped without serious injuries.

2 | Work with a partner. Discuss your reactions to the stories and compare the values you identified for each person.

3 | Tell your partner a story about your personal hero or a person who inspired you in some way. What did this person do? What values does the person have?

Chapter 8

American Values Today

1 GETTING STARTED

In this section, you will read some information about the contrasting values of different groups of Americans. You will also listen to information about a young generation of Americans known as Generation Y.

READING AND THINKING ABOUT THE TOPIC

1 | Read the following passage.

Most Americans today believe in traditional values like the importance of freedom and hard work. However, different groups do not always value these things equally. There are often differences of opinion between generations because of their different life experiences. For example, the *Baby Boomers* – people born between the end of World War II and the mid-1960s – had different experiences from *Generation X*, people born between the mid-1960s and the 1970s, or *Generation Y*, people born during the late 1970s and the 1980s. Experts do not agree on the exact beginning and ending years of these generations, but it is certain that events and technological innovations during these people's lives shaped their values in different ways.

Like people all over the world, Americans do not all share the same political views. Some are more *conservative*, meaning that they tend to believe in keeping traditional cultural and religious values and oppose sudden change. Other Americans are more *liberal*, meaning that they tend to favor reform and progress more than tradition. These different political philosophies often lead to disagreements among Americans about important issues, such as the role of government, taxes, and immigration.

2 Answer the following questions according to the information in the passage:

  1 What are the three generations of Americans that the passage describes?

  2 Why do these three generations often have different values?

  3 What do conservatives tend to believe? What beliefs do liberals tend to share?

3 Read these questions and share your responses with a partner:

  1 Do you think young people always have different values than older people?

  2 Are there some values that you think will never change? If so, what are they? Why won't they change?

SHARING YOUR KNOWLEDGE

Baby Boomer   Generation X   Generation Y

1 Look at the pictures above. Which of the following items were important (or started to become important) when these people were young? Write *BB* (Baby Boomer), *X* (Generation X), or *Y* (Generation Y) on the lines.

1 Important event
     _____ **a** The World Trade Center in New York was attacked.
     _____ **b** The Soviet Union broke up, and the Berlin Wall fell.
     _____ **c** The Vietnam War took place.

2 Important music and musicians
     _____ **a** rock 'n' roll, the Beatles
     _____ **b** hip-hop, OutKast
     _____ **c** punk rock, Madonna

3 Important technology
     _____ **a** iPods
     _____ **b** TVs
     _____ **c** computers

2 As a class, discuss the following questions:

  1 What additional information do you know about these three generations?

  2 How do you think the different experiences of these generations affected their values?

🎧 LISTENING FOR SPECIFIC INFORMATION

1 You will hear a conversation about Generation Y. Look at the illustration above and read the list of information you need to listen for in the left column of the chart below. Then work with a partner and try to predict the information you will hear.

Information to listen for	Notes
Size of Generation Y	
Percentage of U.S. population	
Six times as big as:	
Values of Generation Y	

2 Listen to the conversation and take notes in the right column. ▶ **PLAY**

3 Work with a partner and compare your answers. Then discuss the following questions:

  1 Are you, or someone you know well, a member of Generation Y? Do you or the other person you know have the same values as the man in the conversation?

  2 What are some other values of this generation?

  3 Do Generation Y-ers in other countries you know about have the same values as the man in the conversation?

  4 What problems do members of Generation Y face?

2 AMERICAN VOICES: Rosiane, Dan-el, Christine, and Sandy

In this section, you will hear several Americans talking about their values. First, you will listen to three young adults – Rosiane, Dan-el, and Christine – talk about differences between their values and the values of their parents. Then you will hear an interview with Sandy, who is in her 50s, about values and behavior that young people need in order to succeed in the workplace.

BEFORE THE INTERVIEWS

SHARING YOUR OPINION

What are your most important values? Are they the same as your parents' or different? Fill in the Venn diagram below with examples of your values, your parents' values, and values that you and your parents share. Then compare your answers in small groups.

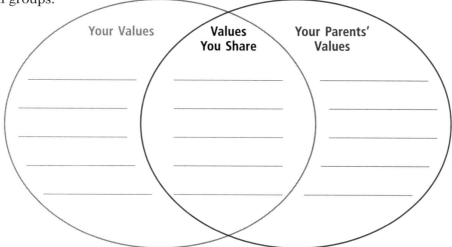

INTERVIEW WITH ROSIANE, DAN-EL, AND CHRISTINE: Differences in values between parents and children

Here are some words and phrases from the interview printed in **bold** and given in the context in which you will hear them. They are followed by definitions.

They wanted me to . . . have kids, so that they could help **bring up** the grandchildren: *raise*

What do your parents think about your **choices**?: *the decisions you made*

I think **I see eye to eye** with my parents: *agree with*

I agree with my parents that children need strong **discipline**: *rules and punishment if the rules are broken*

My parents' generation believes in **spanking** children: *physically punishing, hitting*

I think . . . traveling makes you more **open-minded**: *tolerant, able to accept different opinions*

⋒ DRAWING INFERENCES

Rosiane

Dan-el

Christine

1 | Read the questions below. Then listen to the interviews and write *R* (Rosiane), *D* (Dan-el), or *C* (Christine) on the lines. After listening, check your answers with a partner. ▶ **PLAY**

1 Who thinks it is important to . . .

_____ **a** be independent?

_____ **b** travel?

_____ **c** discipline children?

_____ **d** live abroad?

_____ **e** find a career before getting married?

_____ **f** get an education?

2 Whose parents wanted their child to . . .

_____ **a** get married at a young age?

_____ **b** respect other people?

_____ **c** stay in the town where they live?

2 | Work with a partner. Read the e-mails below and discuss which of the following people might have written them. Put the name of the person in the blank.

- Rosiane
- Rosiane's mother/father
- Dan-el
- Dan-el's mother/father
- Christine
- Christine's mother/father

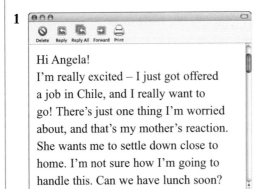

1

> Delete Reply Reply All Forward Print
>
> Hi Angela!
> I'm really excited – I just got offered a job in Chile, and I really want to go! There's just one thing I'm worried about, and that's my mother's reaction. She wants me to settle down close to home. I'm not sure how I'm going to handle this. Can we have lunch soon?

_____

2

> Delete Reply Reply All Forward Print
>
> Hello, Paul dear,
> How are you? I hear you've been having some trouble with the children. You probably don't want my advice, but I think you're too easy on them. You really have to be firm so that they'll respect you and do what you say. That's the way we raised you, Paul, and you turned out beautifully. Well, that's my advice. Take care of yourself. And don't be afraid to let the children know that you're the boss!

_____

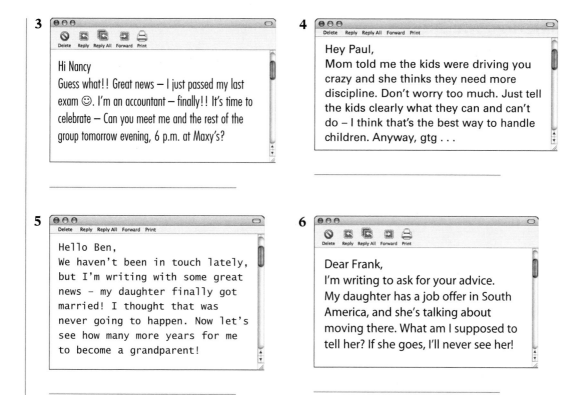

3 | Hi Nancy
Guess what!! Great news — I just passed my last exam ☺. I'm an accountant — finally!! It's time to celebrate — Can you meet me and the rest of the group tomorrow evening, 6 p.m. at Maxy's?

4 | Hey Paul,
Mom told me the kids were driving you crazy and she thinks they need more discipline. Don't worry too much. Just tell the kids clearly what they can and can't do – I think that's the best way to handle children. Anyway, gtg . . .

5 | Hello Ben,
We haven't been in touch lately, but I'm writing with some great news – my daughter finally got married! I thought that was never going to happen. Now let's see how many more years for me to become a grandparent!

6 | Dear Frank,
I'm writing to ask for your advice. My daughter has a job offer in South America, and she's talking about moving there. What am I supposed to tell her? If she goes, I'll never see her!

3 | Discuss this question with your partner: Which values do the writers of the e-mails demonstrate?

INTERVIEW WITH SANDY: Values in the workplace

Here are some words and phrases from the interview with Sandy printed in **bold** and given in the context in which you will hear them. They are followed by definitions.

I find that sometimes, students don't respect **deadlines**: *the date when a task or an assignment must be completed*

They think: "Well, I don't have to **submit** my paper on time": *give the paper to the professor*

They have to learn that that is not **acceptable**: *satisfactory*

You go to the **dealer**, and everything is all paid for: *car salesperson*

You're going to be really **upset**: *angry and unhappy*

They want to **stand out**: *be special, better than anyone else*

You don't work in **isolation**: *alone*

Don't you think individual **effort** is important?: *activity that you need in order to achieve something*

🎧 LISTENING FOR SPECIFIC INFORMATION

1 Read the questions below before you listen to the interview with Sandy. Then listen and take notes on the answers. **▶ PLAY**

1 What is Sandy's job? _____

_____

2 What question does she ask her students? _____

_____

3 Why does she say it is important for students to respect deadlines? _____

_____

4 What story does she tell to show them the importance of time? _____

_____

5 What is the second value she teaches them, and why is it important? _____

_____

6 Which examples does she give of the importance of professionalism? _____

_____

2 Work with a partner and compare answers.

ROLE PLAYING

1 With your partner, read the comments Sandy hears from students who come to talk to her in her office. Discuss how she would probably respond.

a "Good morning, Professor. I'm sorry to bother you. I know you've assigned a group project for next week, but I prefer to work alone. Is that possible?"

b "Hello, Professor, I have a question I need to ask you. I'm almost finished with my term paper, but I need a little bit more time. Could I please turn it in a few days late?"

c "Hey, Prof. Listen, I'm really sorry, but I won't be able to make it to class this afternoon 'cos you know, uh, something's turned up. But . . . uh . . . I'll be there next week, OK?"

Sandy

2 Practice role playing the conversations with your partner. You can expand on the conversation and add more details. Then choose one of your role plays and perform it for another pair of students. Listen as they do their role play for you.

AFTER THE INTERVIEWS

SHARING YOUR OPINION

1 Read the following statements. For each statement, decide whether you strongly agree, agree, aren't sure, disagree, or strongly disagree. Circle the words that show your opinion. Make notes about your reasons.

1 It is important for both men and women to have a career before getting married.

strongly agree   agree   not sure   disagree   strongly disagree

Reason: _____

2 Young adults should follow their parents' advice about important decisions in their lives.

strongly agree   agree   not sure   disagree   strongly disagree

Reason: _____

3 It is important for people to travel to other countries.

strongly agree   agree   not sure   disagree   strongly disagree

Reason: _____

4 Children need strong discipline.

strongly agree   agree   not sure   disagree   strongly disagree

Reason: _____

5 It should be against the law to spank children.

strongly agree   agree   not sure   disagree   strongly disagree

Reason: _____

6 Cooperation is more important than individual effort in the workplace.

strongly agree   agree   not sure   disagree   strongly disagree

Reason: _____

2 Work with a partner and explain your responses.

3 IN YOUR OWN VOICE

In this section, you will conduct a short survey to find out what people you know think is important in a job. Then you will share your findings with a small group.

CONDUCTING A SURVEY

1 Read the following passage.

> A survey done by Charlotte and Laura Shelton for their book *The NeXt Generation* (2005) examined the opinions of women belonging to Generation X. They wanted to know what women of this age considered important in a good job. They found that younger workers and older workers valued different things. The top three things women in Generation X valued were good relationships with their colleagues, interesting jobs, and opportunities to learn. They were less interested in high salaries and power, which were important job characteristics for Baby Boomers.

2 Interview at least three people outside your class. Find at least one person from each of the three generations discussed in this chapter: Baby Boomers, Generation X, and Generation Y. Follow these steps:

1 Use the chart on the next page for your survey, or make a chart of your own. (You will have to make your own chart if you survey more than three people.)

2 Circle "Male" or "Female" for each interviewee. Then ask each person what he or she thinks is important in a good job. For each statement in the left column, ask if the person strongly agrees (A+), agrees (A), isn't sure (?), disagrees (D), or strongly disagrees (D+). Here is a way to start:

> *Excuse me. I'm conducting a survey for my English class. It's about what qualities in a job people feel are important. Do you have time to answer a few questions for me?*

3 Check [✔] each response in the appropriate column.

4 Ask follow-up questions to get details about why the interviewees have their opinions. For example, you could say:

> *Why do you like to work independently?*
> or
> *Could you explain why you strongly disagree with . . . ?*

Take notes on how the interviewees reply to your follow-up questions.

Important Characteristics of a Good Job															
In my job, it is important to have . . .	Person 1: Baby Boomer					Person 2: Generation X					Person 3: Generation Y				
	Male / Female					Male / Female					Male / Female				
	A+	A	?	D	D+	A+	A	?	D	D+	A+	A	?	D	D+
1 good relationships with other workers.															
2 interesting work to do.															
3 a good salary.															
4 job security (meaning that you can't easily lose your job).															
5 long vacations.															
6 opportunities to learn.															
7 chances to work independently.															

Notes:

3 Answer the following questions:

1 Did you find any differences between the responses of older and younger people? What were they?

2 Which three items did all the interviewees value most? Were they similar to or different from the results of the Shelton survey described on the previous page?

3 What was the most interesting answer the speakers gave to your follow-up questions?

4 Work in small groups and compare your answers.

4 ACADEMIC LISTENING AND NOTE TAKING: Conservative and Liberal Values in American Politics

In this section, you will hear and take notes on a two-part lecture by Professor Jason Rose. The title of his lecture is *Conservative and Liberal Values in American Politics.* Professor Rose will discuss these values and their relationship to the two main political parties in the United States.

BEFORE THE LECTURE

BUILDING BACKGROUND KNOWLEDGE

1 In this task, you will learn some facts about the two main political parties in the United States, the Democratic Party and the Republican Party.

Work with a partner.
Partner A, look at the chart below on this page.
Partner B, look at the chart at the top of the next page.

2 Ask your partner questions about the information that is missing from your chart. Fill in the blanks with information your partner gives you. Then answer your partner's questions. Here is an example:

A: What is the color of the Republican Party?
B: Red. What is the symbol of the Democratic Party?
A: A donkey.

Partner A

Facts	Democratic Party	Republican Party
Political philosophy	Liberalism	
Color	Blue	
Symbol	Donkey	
Web site	www.democrats.org	
Interesting fact	the first party to nominate a woman for Vice President	
Some well-known Presidents	Bill Clinton Lyndon Johnson John F. Kennedy Franklin D. Roosevelt	

Partner B

Facts	Republican Party	Democratic Party
Political philosophy	Conservatism	
Color	Red	
Symbol	Elephant	
Web site	www.gop.com	
Interesting fact	commonly called the GOP (Grand Old Party)	
Some well-known Presidents	George W. Bush Ronald Reagan Richard Nixon	

🎧 NOTE TAKING: LISTENING FOR GENERAL STATEMENTS

It is common in a short lecture for the speaker to make general statements about a topic because there is not enough time to give detailed information. Here are some words and phrases that are often used to make general statements:

generally	*in general*	*commonly*	*many*
most	*often*	*typically*	*usually*

1 | Read the statements below. Notice that they do not use any of the words and phrases from the box.

_____ **1** But even though people's values are very diverse, the strongest voices in American politics today do fall into two groups – conservative and liberal.

_____ **2** Conservatives put a strong emphasis on personal responsibility.

_____ **3** Liberals, on the other hand, think the government should be very active in fixing social problems like poverty and illness.

_____ **4** Conservatives think government is too big and expensive.

_____ **5** Conservatives believe that the government should stay out of the way of business.

_____ **6** Liberals believe that government should control and regulate business through strict laws or taxes.

_____ **7** The U.S. has two main political parties, so in an election, voters choose between the Republicans and the Democrats.

2 | Now listen to the statements with words and phrases that signal general statements. Write the signal word or phrase you hear next to each statement in step 1. ▶ PLAY

3 | Work with a partner and compare your answers. Discuss the difference in meaning between the sentences in step 1 and in step 2.

LECTURE, PART ONE: Conservative and Liberal Values

GUESSING VOCABULARY FROM CONTEXT

1 | The following items contain important vocabulary from Part One of the lecture. Work with a partner. Using the context and your knowledge of related words, take turns trying to guess the meanings of the words in bold.

_____ **1** Let me outline for you some basic differences between conservatives and liberals in three areas: the role of the government, taxes, and government **regulation** of business.

_____ **2** Conservatives usually put a strong **emphasis** on personal responsibility.

_____ **3** They don't believe it's the government's responsibility to pay for social programs that guarantee things like a **minimum wage**.

_____ **4** Most liberals . . . think the government should be very active in fixing social problems like **poverty** and illness.

_____ **5** The government . . . shouldn't **interfere** too much in the way business works.

_____ **6** They think entrepreneurs won't care about their workers or their customers or the **environment**.

_____ **7** They'll only care about their own **profits**.

2 | Work with your partner. Match the vocabulary terms with their definitions by writing the letter of each definition below in the blank next to the sentence or phrase containing the correct term in step 1. Check your answers in a dictionary if necessary.

   a special attention that is given to something because it is important
   b being poor
   c money that a business makes
   d participate without being wanted or asked to do so
   e control of, rules on
   f the lowest salary that a business is allowed by law to pay its employees
   g the natural world around us, nature

∩ NOTE TAKING: TAKING NOTES IN A POINT-BY-POINT FORMAT

When lecturers compare two or more groups, they often use a "point-by-point" format to organize their ideas. Here is an example:

Topics (points):
1. Attitudes toward marriage
2. Attitudes about money
3. Voting patterns

Groups compared:
– Baby Boomers
– Generation Y

– Baby Boomers
– Generation Y

– Baby Boomers
– Generation Y

1 Look at the incomplete notes for Part One of the lecture. Predict the information you need to listen for.

Conserv./Lib. Values

1. Role of gov't

   Conserv: Not gov't resp. to pay for social progs.
   Lib: Gov't. should fix soc. prob's like poverty + illness

2. _____ _____

3. _____ _____

   Ex: _____

2 Now listen to Part One of the lecture and take notes on your own paper. Use a point-by-point format like the one above. ▶ PLAY

3 Work with a partner and compare your notes. Then use your notes to fill in the missing information in step 1.

LECTURE, PART TWO: Values and Political Parties

GUESSING VOCABULARY FROM CONTEXT

1 | The following items contain important vocabulary from Part Two of the lecture. Work with a partner. Using the context and your knowledge of related words, take turns trying to guess the meanings of the words in **bold**.

_____ **1** There has been a huge change in people's **voting patterns**.

_____ **2** Twenty years later, there was a **dramatic** change.

_____ **3** In fact, the country was **split down the middle**.

_____ **4** Voters are responding to high **employment** or **unemployment**.

_____ **5** A strong economy helped Ronald Reagan get elected for a second **term** in 1984.

_____ **6** The attack of September 11, 2001 was probably a factor in George W. Bush's **reelection** in 2004.

_____ **7** I want to **emphasize** that I've been discussing American political values and the political system in a very general way.

_____ **8** In practice, many people are not **strict** conservatives or liberals.

_____ **9** All 50 states are actually different shades of **purple** . . .

2 | Work with your partner. Match the vocabulary terms with their definitions by writing the letter of each definition below in the blank next to the sentence or phrase containing the correct term in step 1. Check your answers in a dictionary if necessary.

a divided half and half
b the usual or normal way that most people vote
c the percentage of people who have (or don't have) work
d a mixture of red and blue
e say strongly, stress
f 100 percent, completely
g large and very noticeable
h win an election for the second time
i the period of time an elected official serves

🎧 NOTE TAKING: USING A HANDOUT TO HELP YOU TAKE NOTES

Lecturers sometimes give students handouts to illustrate their lectures or provide additional information. If you receive a handout, read it before the lecture. Use it to make predictions about the lecture, look up new vocabulary, or write comments or questions about parts that you do not understand.

1 | Look at the handout on the next page that Professor Rose gave to his students. Then study the incomplete notes for Part One of the lecture below the handout. Predict the information you need to listen for.

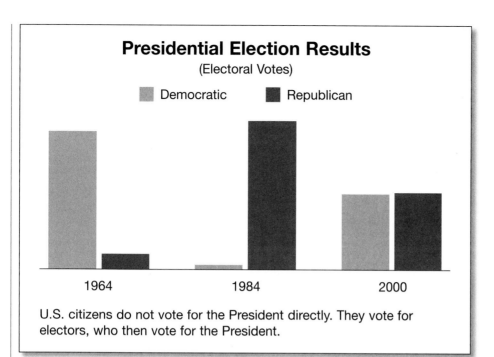

Presidential Election Results
(Electoral Votes)

Democratic   Republican

1964   1984   2000

U.S. citizens do not vote for the President directly. They vote for electors, who then vote for the President.

Values + Pol. Parties

I. Intro
   A. U.S. has 2-party system
   B. In gen: Repub = conserv
            Dem = lib
   C. But: ideas change over time

II. Election results
   A. 1964: _____
   B. 1984: _____
   C. 2000: _____

III. _____
_____
_____
_____

IV. Conc: _____

2 | Listen to Part Two of the lecture and take notes on your own paper. ▶ PLAY

3 | Compare your notes with a partner. Then use your notes to fill in the missing information in step 1.

AFTER THE LECTURE

SHARING YOUR OPINION

1 │ Are you more liberal or more conservative? Take the quiz below to find out! Read each statement and circle *Agree, Not Sure,* or *Disagree* to indicate your opinions.

1 We must protect our natural resources (forests, rivers, lakes, etc.), even if this means we must limit business activities in these areas.

    Agree   Not sure   Disagree

2 The government should restrict immigration to the United States.

    Agree   Not sure   Disagree

3 Businesses should give preference to members of minority groups in their employment policies because they were treated unfairly in the past.

    Agree   Not sure   Disagree

4 Carrying a gun is an American right.

    Agree   Not sure   Disagree

5 It is important for the government to provide health care, even if this means increasing taxes.

    Agree   Not sure   Disagree

6 In some cases, death is the right punishment for criminals.

    Agree   Not sure   Disagree

7 The government should provide equal access to a good education for all its citizens.

    Agree   Not sure   Disagree

8 Taxes should be cut if it will help the economy to grow.

    Agree   Not sure   Disagree

2 │ Score your quiz. Give yourself points and place an *X* on the scale to show how your views compare with the views of liberal and conservative Americans.

    Odd numbers (1, 3, 5, 7):   Agree = 0, Not sure = 1, Disagree = 2
    Even numbers (2, 4, 6, 8): Agree = 2, Not sure = 1, Disagree = 0

0   **16**
──
More liberal   More conservative

3 │ Work with a partner or small group. Compare and discuss your responses to the statements in step 1.

Spotlight on Culture

In this unit, you will focus on different aspects of American culture and society. Chapter 9 deals with American innovations in a variety of areas. You will hear interviews about innovations in digital technology, sports, and movies. The subject of the lecture is the blues and country music, two musical genres, or styles, that originated in the United States. The topic of Chapter 10 is global transformations, that is, the process of change that occurs when products or practices that originated in one country become popular in other countries. The interviews in this chapter provide examples of such transformations in health practices, cars, and food. The lecture is about the globalization of American slang.

American Innovations

Chapter **9**

1 GETTING STARTED

In this section, you will read about the spirit of innovation in the United States. You will also listen as two people discuss the origins of various inventions and innovations.

READING AND THINKING ABOUT THE TOPIC

1 | Read the following passage.

The term *innovation* includes the invention of new products or systems, changes to existing products or systems, and the introduction of different and original ways of looking at things.

Americans, who value risk taking and independence, also value innovation greatly. From the beginning of the nation through modern times, innovation has affected many areas of life in the United States. Today, innovations in digital media have a particular impact on the daily life of Americans. The most obvious example is the Internet – an American innovation that has dramatically changed the way people live, work, and study.

Thanks to the spirit of innovation, Americans have introduced new sports, media, and music to the world. For example, people from all countries now watch baseball on TV, enjoy movies made in Hollywood, and listen to jazz and hip-hop.

2 Answer the following questions according to the information in the passage:

   1 What is the relationship between an invention and an innovation?

   2 In what aspects of life do Americans value innovation?

3 Read these questions and share your responses with a partner:

   1 What qualities do you think innovative people have?

   2 Do the innovations mentioned in the passage affect your life? In what ways?

🎧 LISTENING FOR SPECIFIC INFORMATION

1 UKTV, one of Britain's largest television channels, made a list of the Top Ten Modern Inventions and posted it online in 2006. Work with a partner and look at the items below. Guess the country where each item was invented and the year the invention appeared. (Hint: Seven of the products were invented in the United States.)

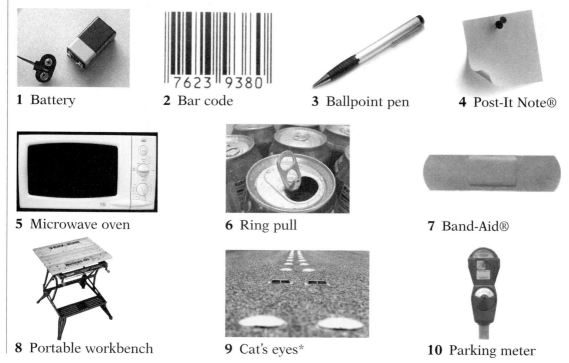

| **1** Battery | **2** Bar code | **3** Ballpoint pen | **4** Post-It Note® |

| **5** Microwave oven | **6** Ring pull | **7** Band-Aid® |

| **8** Portable workbench | **9** Cat's eyes* | **10** Parking meter |

2 Now listen. Under each picture, write the year when and country where the item was invented. ▶ PLAY

3 Work with a partner and compare answers. Then discuss the following questions regarding each invention on the list:

   1 Do you, your family, or friends make use of this invention?

   2 Do you agree that this item should be on the list of top ten inventions? Why or why not?

   3 Why do you think so many items on the list were invented in the United States?

---

* Glass pieces that are set in the road and shine in the dark to show drivers the way.

2 AMERICAN VOICES: Cristina, Victor, Ronnie, and Mara

In this section, you will hear four Americans talk about American innovations. First, Cristina and Victor will talk about the impact of digital technology on their lives, and then Ronnie and Mara will discuss American innovations in sports and movies.

BEFORE THE INTERVIEWS

SHARING YOUR OPINION

Work with a partner. Read this list of innovations and answer the questions that follow:

> MP3 player
> laptop
> cell phone
> CD
> digital camera
> inline skates
> Heelys
> skateboard
> snowboard

1 Do you use these items? How often?

2 Why are these items innovations? Did any of them replace earlier items?

BUILDING BACKGROUND KNOWLEDGE

The terms on the left are used in the interviews. Match each term with its definition.

_____ **1** go online	**a** transfer or copy information, images, or music from the Internet to a computer or other electronic device
_____ **2** post	**b** computer files that contain audio material
_____ **3** links	**c** get connected to e-mail or the Internet
_____ **4** sound files	**d** send a message to be published on an Internet site
_____ **5** download	**e** unwanted e-mail messages, especially advertisements
_____ **6** spam	**f** a digital audio program that is posted online and can be downloaded
_____ **7** podcast	**g** "addresses" that computer users can use to connect to Internet pages by clicking on them

INTERVIEW WITH CRISTINA AND VICTOR: Using digital technology

Here are some words and phrases from the interviews printed in **bold** and given in the context in which you will hear them. They are followed by definitions.

Some colleagues **took me aside**: *talked to me privately*

I've become quite **proficient**: *good at doing something*

Recently, I **upgraded** to a really powerful computer: *got a newer, better one*

All this technology has some **drawbacks**: *disadvantages*

I find them very annoying and **intrusive**: *interfering with my life*

I use [my computer] . . . to **IM** my friends: *send an Instant Message to*

All the readings and **syllabi** are online: *course outlines (singular: syllabus)*

I'm online **24/7**: *all the time (24 hours a day, 7 days a week)*

☊ ANSWERING MULTIPLE CHOICE QUESTIONS

1 | Read the following questions before you listen to the interview with Cristina and Victor:

Cristina

1 When did Cristina first start using computers?
a as a young child
b in high school
c as an adult

2 When did she first start to use e-mail?
a as soon as it was invented
b in her last job
c she doesn't use e-mail

3 Why did Cristina buy an iPod?
a She wanted to store photos on it.
b She wanted to download music from the Internet.
c She wanted to give one to her friend.

4 Cristina uses computers in all of the following ways, except:
a to do research
b to post her lectures online
c for entertainment

5 Cristina doesn't own a cell phone for the following reasons, except:
a they take away your privacy
b they're annoying
c they're expensive

Victor

6 How important is digital technology in Victor's life?

   a not very important

   b quite important

   c extremely important

7 Victor got his first laptop when he was

   a 18

   b 11

   c 20

8 He needs a computer at college because

   a he needs to write research papers

   b the readings and syllabi are online

   c the professors won't accept handwritten work

9 Why does Victor sometimes prefer pencil and paper?

   a It helps him think more clearly.

   b The classrooms do not have wireless access.

   c His computer often breaks down.

10 What is a disadvantage of using computers, according to Victor?

   a computer viruses

   b back problems

   c spam

2 | Now listen to the interview with Cristina and Victor. Circle the letter of the correct answer to each question above. Then work with a partner and compare answers.
▶ PLAY

INTERVIEW WITH RONNIE AND MARA: *Innovations in sports and movies*

Here are some words and phrases from the interview with Ronnie and Mara printed in **bold** and given in the context in which you will hear them. They are followed by definitions.

Snowboarding is really, really fast. . . . And plus, it's kind of **trendy**: *fashionable, something that many people are doing*

You have to have special equipment . . . [and that] can get **pretty** expensive: *quite, very*

A lot of people get **injured** trying [extreme sports]: *hurt*

[Black-and-white films] sometimes have better stories than the modern **blockbusters**: *best sellers*

I find that sometimes the **plots** . . . aren't all that good: *the main events of the stories*

DRAWING INFERENCES

1 │ Read the statements about Ronnie and Mara below.

Ronnie

Ronnie

_____ 1 Ronnie is good at sports.

_____ 2 Ronnie enjoys team sports more than individual sports.

_____ 3 Ronnie watches a lot of TV.

_____ 4 Ronnie is concerned about safety.

_____ 5 Ronnie is going to buy a snowboard.

Mara

_____ 6 Mara rents a lot of movies.

_____ 7 Mara knows a lot about the way movies are made.

_____ 8 Mara often recommends films to her friends.

_____ 9 Mara prefers movies with serious themes.

_____ 10 Mara thinks that movies without special effects are boring.

Mara

2 │ Now listen to the interview. ▶ **PLAY**

3 │ For each statement in step 1, decide if it is *L* (likely), *U* (unlikely), or *?* (hard to say) that the statement is true. Write *L*, *U*, or *?* next to each statement.

Forrest Gump

Shrek

AFTER THE INTERVIEWS

DISCUSSING PROS AND CONS

Pros and *cons* are arguments for (pro) or against (con) something. They are similar to advantages and disadvantages. Discussing pros and cons often requires expressions that can show contrast, such as *but, yet, although, even though,* and *on the other hand*. Read the following sentences and notice how these expressions are used:

- Powerful computers are convenient, *but/yet* they are often expensive.
- *Although/Even though* snowboarding looks easy, it is physically demanding.
- Thanks to special effects, modern movies are fascinating to watch. *On the other hand,* sometimes the stories aren't very interesting.

1 The interviewees discussed advantages and disadvantages of the innovations listed in the chart below. Fill in the chart with the pros and cons they mentioned. Add your own ideas as well. If you need more space, make a larger chart on separate paper.

Speaker	Innovation	Pros	Cons
Cristina	Computer	Search engines help her find information quickly.	
	MP3 player (iPod)		
	Cell phone		
Victor	Computer (laptop)		
Ronnie	Extreme sports		
Mara	Special effects		

2 Work in groups of four. Two students should present the pros of an innovation. The others should present the cons. Change positions after each item you discuss. Be sure to use expressions of contrast from the box at the top of the page.

Example
A: For Cristina, one of the advantages of computers is that she can use search engines to find information quickly.
B: That's true, but on the other hand, computers are very expensive, and the technology gets old very fast.

3 IN YOUR OWN VOICE

In this section, you will conduct research on American innovations, make a handout showing what you have found, and present your research to your classmates.

CONDUCTING RESEARCH

1 | Below is a list of American innovations. Work with a partner and write each item in its proper category or categories in the chart. Use a dictionary if necessary.

- Scotch® tape
- artificial heart
- assembly-line production
- blues
- coffee pot
- cowboy boots
- jazz
- jeans
- lightbulb
- power tools
- robotic surgery
- sewing machine

Clothing	Household Items	Medicine
Music	**Industry**	**Office Equipment**

2 | With your partner, choose one item from the chart. Do research online or in a library to find the answers to the following questions:

- Who invented this product, practice, or process?
- What is its importance or appeal?
- What was used before it was invented?
- What interesting story can you find about this item?
- Where did you find your information?

3 | Working together, organize your research and make a handout or poster of the information you found.

4 | Make a presentation to the class that includes the answers to the questions in step 2. Refer to your handout or poster as you speak.

ACADEMIC LISTENING AND NOTE TAKING: The Blues and Country Music: Two American Musical Genres

In this section, you will hear and take notes on a two-part lecture by Professor Daniel Erker called *The Blues and Country Music: Two American Musical Genres*. Professor Erker will talk about these two genres, or styles, of traditional American music. He will also play musical examples with one of his colleagues from their band The Jones Street Boys.

BEFORE THE LECTURE

SHARING YOUR KNOWLEDGE

1 | Work with a partner. Classify these words that relate to the blues or country music by putting them in the correct column in the chart below.

Appalachia   country   guitar   piano
banjo   cruelty   harmonica   Robert Johnson
bass   devotion   loyalty   saxophone
Bessie Smith   Dixie Chicks lost love   violin
blues   drums   Mississippi Delta   Willie Nelson

Genres	Places of origin	Themes	Instruments	Musicians
blues				

2 | Look at these pictures of famous blues and country singers and groups. As a class, answer the following questions:

1 Can you identify these musicians? Do you know which type of music they perform? (Check the bottom of page 140 for the answers)

2 Have you ever heard music by these musicians? If so, do you like it? Why or why not?

⌒ NOTE TAKING: LISTENING FOR SIMILARITIES AND DIFFERENCES

> There are many ways of talking about similarities and differences in English. Study the examples below. The words in **bold** signal a similarity or a difference.
>
> **Similarities**
>
> **Both** jazz and blues originated in the United States.
>
> **Like** jazz, hip-hop has its roots in African-American culture.
>
> There are many **similarities between** jazz and blues.
>
> Rock and modern country music use many of the **same** instruments.
>
> **Differences**
>
> **Unlike** country music fans, reggaeton fans live mostly in urban areas.
>
> **While/Whereas** jazz uses a variety of instruments, blues relies strongly on guitars.
>
> Rock 'n' roll and rap are totally **different**. They are quite **distinct**.

1 | The following sentences are from the lecture. Predict which words are missing. Use words from the box above and your own ideas to help you.

  1 _____ the blues, country also developed as a unique musical genre.

  2 The other big _____ to the blues is that country is a uniquely American genre.

  3 But that's where the _____ end because of course, blues and country are very _____.

  4 So country music came from a _____ geographic area _____ the blues.

  5 _____ country music traditionally had some of the _____ sad themes as the blues, it included positive themes, too.

  6 The third _____, of course, is that country sounds very _____ from the blues.

  7 _____ the blues, country is often played by groups of musicians and singers, not just one.

2 | Now listen to the excerpts from the lecture and fill in the words you hear. Then work with a partner and compare answers. ▶ PLAY

LECTURE, PART ONE: The Blues

GUESSING VOCABULARY FROM CONTEXT

1 | The items at the top of the following page contain important vocabulary from Part One of the lecture. Work with a partner. Using the context and your knowledge of related words, take turns trying to guess the meaning of the words in **bold**.

_____ 1 "Having the blues" means that a person is feeling sad, troubled, or **melancholy**.

_____ 2 The blues is a unique musical genre, and by that I mean . . . well, the **elements** it includes. . . .

_____ 3 The blues . . . is played by a **lone** bluesman. . . .

_____ 4 . . . singing about lost love, poverty, and the **cruelty** of life.

_____ 5 During the twentieth century, it became more **commercialized**.

2 Work with your partner. Match the vocabulary terms with their definitions by writing the letter of each definition below in the blank next to the sentence or phrase containing the correct term in step 1. Check your answers in a dictionary if necessary.

a sad and nostalgic
b painfulness, unfairness
c different parts
d single, one person
e made in such a way that selling it will be profitable

🎧 NOTE TAKING: CHOOSING A FORMAT FOR YOUR NOTES

By now you have learned several formats for taking notes. Choosing a format is a very individual choice, and different formats work well for different people at different times. Often the best format to use depends on the organization of the lecture you are hearing. For example:

A chart: If there are different categories of information, a chart can help you to organize the details effectively.

Columns: Columns are helpful if you are comparing two things or two sets of information.

A map: Maps provide a visual representation of the relationships between different ideas. They are useful for grouping related information when the sequence is not important.

An outline: Outlines are the clearest way to show the sequence of information and the relationship between main ideas and different levels of details.

1 Listen to the introduction to the lecture and use it to decide which format you want to take your notes in. Choose from one of the four formats on the next page. **▶ PLAY**

Answers to step 2, question 1:
1 Willie Nelson, country music 2 Robert Johnson, blues
3 Bessie Smith, blues 4 Dixie Chicks, country music

Chart

2 Am. Musical Genres

	Blues	Country
Origin		
Musical elements		
Famous musicians		

Columns

2 Am. Musical Genres

Blues	Country
Origin	Origin
Musical elements	Musical elements
Famous musicians	Famous musicians

Map

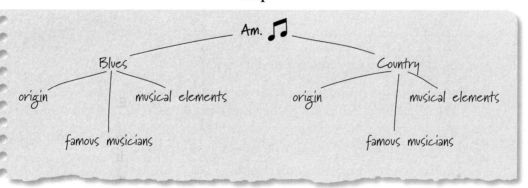

Am. ♫

Blues — origin, musical elements, famous musicians

Country — origin, musical elements, famous musicians

Outline

Two Genres of Am. ♫

I. Blues
   A. Origin
   B. Musical elements
   C. Famous musicians

II. Country
   A. Origin
   B. Musical elements
   C. Famous musicians

2 Listen to Part One of the lecture. Using the format that you have chosen, take notes using your own paper. ▶ PLAY

3 Work with a partner and clarify your notes. Then copy your notes neatly using the format you prefer.

LECTURE, PART TWO: Country Music

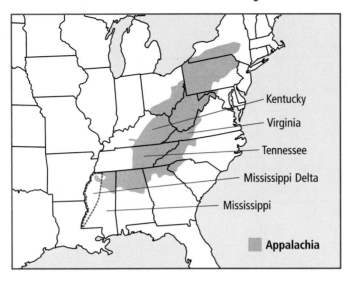

GUESSING VOCABULARY FROM CONTEXT

1 The following items contain important vocabulary from Part Two of the lecture. Work with a partner. Using the context and your knowledge of related words, take turns trying to guess the meanings of the words in bold.

_____ **1** It was influenced by . . . **folk music** from Britain.

_____ **2** It was played by the **descendents** of white European immigrants.

_____ **3** [They] lived in **rural** areas.

_____ **4** It included positive themes, too, like the musicians' **devotion** to their homes.

_____ **5** . . . singing in **harmony**.

2 Work with your partner. Match the vocabulary terms with their definitions by writing the letter of each definition below in the blank next to the sentence or phrase containing the correct term in step 1. Check your answers in a dictionary if necessary.

a musical notes that contrast with the main tune
b children, grandchildren, great grandchildren, and so on
c areas outside the city; in the country
d traditional songs
e affection and loyalty

NOTE TAKING: CHOOSING A FORMAT FOR YOUR NOTES

1 Listen to Part Two of the lecture and complete the notes you started in Part One.
▶ PLAY

2 Work with a partner and compare your notes. Clarify any information you missed.

3 Revise and copy your notes neatly.

AFTER THE LECTURE

USING YOUR NOTES TO MAKE NOTE CARDS

An effective way to study for tests is to write important information from lectures on note cards. Write each key word, concept, or name on one side of a card. Write the definition or explanation on the other side. You can use the cards to study either alone or with others.

1 With a partner, make note cards that you can use to study for a test. One partner should prepare cards on Part One of the lecture. The other partner should prepare cards on Part Two. Follow the example below.

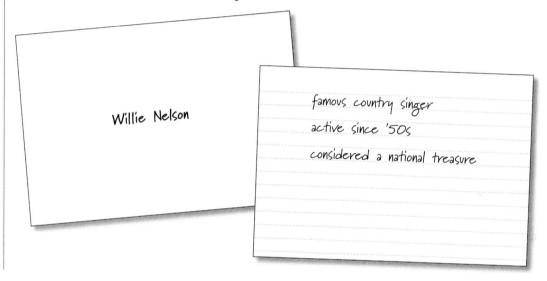

Willie Nelson

famous country singer
active since '50s
considered a national treasure

2 Use the note cards you prepared to quiz your partner. Ask questions based on the information you wrote on the cards, for example: Who was Willie Nelson? When did his musical career begin?

3 Exchange note cards with a partner. Use your partner's cards to study alone. Look at the side of each card containing the key term. Try to identify or explain it. If you need help, check the other side of the card.

Chapter 10

Global Transformations

1 GETTING STARTED

In this section, you will read about globalization and the process of transformation that is often a result of globalization. You will also listen to two people discuss advertisements for products that are available worldwide.

READING AND THINKING ABOUT THE TOPIC

1 | Read the following passage.

The term *globalization* describes the close economic relationship that countries and communities around the world have today. However, it is also used to describe our social, political, and cultural interdependence.

One aspect of globalization is the movement of products and ideas across national boundaries. For example, YouTube, which began in the United States, is a free video sharing Web site that is now so popular worldwide that it was called the "2006 Invention of the Year." The game Sudoku has a different type of history. It was invented by an American in 1979. However, it did not become popular in the United States until after it was published in Japan. The name is a shortened version of a Japanese expression meaning "the digits must occur only once."

As they travel from one country to another, products and ideas often undergo a change, that is, a transformation. Fast food is one example. Although fast foods from the United States have become popular in other countries, changes to these fast foods often take place due to the use of local ingredients. Furthermore, although the use of fast food began in the Unites States, individual countries have created fast-food versions of their own dishes, which are now popular in the United States as well as in other countries around the world.

2 | Answer the following questions according to the information in the passage:

1 What is *globalization*?

2 What is an example of global transformation?

3 | Read these questions and share your responses with a partner:

1 Which products do you use that originated in another country?

2 Do you think that the world will get "smaller" in the future? If so, how?

🎧 LISTENING FOR TONE OF VOICE

Speakers tell you their opinions not only with words but also by their tone of voice. They can indicate surprise, disbelief, anger, and many other emotions by changing their tone. They can also show degrees of their emotions by their tone of voice. In other words, they can show whether an emotion is strong or mild by the amount of stress they put on a word or phrase and the rise or fall of their tone.

1 | Work with a partner. Look at the photos and guess where they were taken.

1

2

Place: _____

Woman's reaction (circle one):

strong surprise / mild surprise

Place: _____

Man's reaction (circle one):

strong surprise / mild surprise

3

4

Place: _____

Woman's reaction (circle one):

strong surprise / mild surprise

Place: _____

Man's reaction (circle one):

strong surprise / mild surprise

2 | Listen to two people discussing the photos. Fill in the blanks with the information you hear and circle the degree of the first speaker's reaction. ▶ **PLAY**

2 AMERICAN VOICES: Adam, María, Lindsay, and Chander

In this section, you will hear four Americans talking about practices and products from other countries that have influenced their lives. First, you will listen to an interview with Adam and María about two health practices that originated in other countries. Then you will hear Lindsay and Chander discuss how cars and food from other countries are an important part of their lives in the United States.

BEFORE THE INTERVIEWS

SHARING YOUR KNOWLEDGE

Work with a partner. Look at the pictures below. They show activities related to health and exercise that are popular in countries other than where they originated. Tell your partner what you know about each activity. Why do you think these activities have become popular in many countries?

1 karate, China

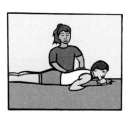

2 shiatsu massage, Japan

3 yoga, India

4 tai chi, China

5 salsa, Caribbean

6 acupuncture, China

7 tango, Argentina

8 chiropractic, United States

INTERVIEW WITH ADAM AND MARIA: *Two health practices*

Here are some words and phrases from the interview with Adam and María printed in **bold** and given in the context in which you will hear them. They are followed by definitions.

An acupuncturist puts **needles** into different parts of your body: *thin pieces of metal with a sharp point at one end*

They can help you **get over** your physical problem: *make it go away*

I decided to try an **alternative** treatment: *not always accepted by medical doctors*

In Asia, acupuncture is considered an **ancient** medical practice: *very old*

But in the U.S., it's become kind of a **luxury** because most health insurance companies don't cover it: *very expensive and not considered to be necessary*

I take a class at my **gym** every Tuesday: *gymnasium, sports center*

It's really **trendy**: *in fashion, being done by lots of people*

I think it's part of the **Hindu religion**: *the main religion of India*

. . . there's a whole **philosophy** behind it: *set of beliefs*

Adam

María

RETELLING WHAT YOU HAVE HEARD

1 | Look at the chart below before you listen to the interview with Adam and María.

Practice	Place of origin	How it is used differently in the United States than in its place of origin
acupuncture		

2 | Now listen to the interview and take notes in the chart. ▶ **PLAY**

3 | Work with a partner and take turns retelling what Adam and María said.

INTERVIEW WITH LINDSAY AND CHANDER: Cars and food

Lindsay

Chander

Here are some words and phrases from the interview printed in **bold** and given in the context in which you will hear them. They are followed by definitions.

In America, people like **automatics**: *cars that change gears without the driver's help*

We serve **authentic** Indian food: *being what it is supposed to be, not fake*

Sometimes we have to change the **recipes** a little bit: *the way the dishes are prepared*

Indian food has certain **spices** that are quite strong: *parts of plants that are used in cooking to give food flavor*

⌒ RETELLING WHAT YOU HAVE HEARD

1 | Look at the chart below before you listen to the interview with Lindsay and Chander.

Item	Place of origin	How it is used differently in the United States than in its place of origin

2 | Now listen to the interview and take notes in the chart. ▶ PLAY

3 | Work with a partner and take turns retelling what Lindsay and Chander said.

AFTER THE INTERVIEWS

DEVELOPING CONVERSATIONS ABOUT A TOPIC

Developing a conversation about a topic is a good way to practice new vocabulary and demonstrate your understanding of the topic.

1 Work in small groups and finish developing these conversations. Use your own paper if you want to make the conversations longer.

a Acupuncture
A: I'm so upset. My mom has started getting allergic to cats, and now she says she won't come to visit me because my roommate has a cat.
B: Did she ever think of trying acupuncture? I heard that can help people with allergies.
A: _____
B: _____

b Yoga
A: Hi, you don't look so good. What's up?
B: Well, I have a backache. I think it's because I'm so stressed out. I'm feeling tense and nervous.
A: Why don't you try yoga? I've heard that's really good for relaxation, and there's a class at the local gym.
B: _____
A: _____

c Cars
A: My car's finally broken down for good. I'm getting a new one.
B: You should get a foreign car. I heard they have some very good deals right now.
A: _____
B: _____

d Food
A: Let's eat out tonight. There are a few new restaurants I'd like to check out.
B: Where do you want to go?
A: Well, there's a new Italian place, or . . . uh . . . let's see. Let's look at the paper here. Oh, or how about a Lebanese restaurant . . . or Thai?
B: _____
A: _____

2 Choose two people from each group to perform one of the conversations in front of the class. Don't look at your notes while you're performing.

3 IN YOUR OWN VOICE

In this section, you will work in a team and then with a partner from a different team to describe and explain items that have become popular worldwide.

SHARING YOUR KNOWLEDGE

As a class, divide into two teams: A and B. Team A: follow the instructions below. Team B: Follow the instructions on page 151.

Instructions for Team A

1 In small groups, try to answer the questions on Board A in as much detail as you can. Then check your answers on page 158. Try to remember the answers so you don't have to look at them again while you're playing the game.

2 Now work with a partner from Team B. Ask your partner from Team B to answer the questions on Board A. Give your partner 1 point for each question he or she gets right (a possible total of 18 points).

3 If your partner can't answer a question, tell him or her the answer. If you know more about the topic, you can add your own information.

BOARD A

BEGIN HERE →

1 Barbie dolls

a What are they?

b T/F: Barbie dolls are based on dolls originally made in Germany.

2 Blue jeans

a What are they?

b T/F: The name *blue jeans* comes from an expression in Polish.

3 Waltz

a What is it?

b T/F: The waltz is a traditional American dance.

8 Hollywood

a What is it?

b T/F: Hollywood is located in Washington, D.C.

9 Rap music

a What is it?

b T/F: Rap music originally comes from the United States.

4 Burrito

a What is it?

b T/F: In English, *burritos* are usually called *tacos*.

7 Soccer

a What is it?

b T/F: FIFA, the International Association of soccer, is based in England.

6 Reggae

a What is it?

b T/F: Reggae originally comes from Jamaica.

5 Video games

a What are they?

b T/F: Video games were invented in Japan.

Instructions for Team B

1   In small groups, try to answer the questions on Board B in as much detail as you can. Then check your answers on page 159. Try to remember the answers so you don't have to look at them again while you're playing the game.

2   Now work with a partner from Team A. Ask your partner from Team A to answer the questions on Board B. Give your partner 1 point for each question he or she gets right (a possible total of 18 points).

3   If your partner can't answer a question, tell him or her the answer. If you know more about the topic, you can add your own information.

BOARD B

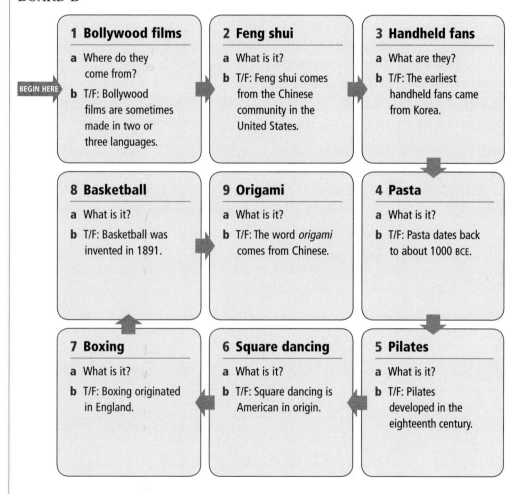

BEGIN HERE

1 Bollywood films
a   Where do they come from?
b   T/F: Bollywood films are sometimes made in two or three languages.

2 Feng shui
a   What is it?
b   T/F: Feng shui comes from the Chinese community in the United States.

3 Handheld fans
a   What are they?
b   T/F: The earliest handheld fans came from Korea.

8 Basketball
a   What is it?
b   T/F: Basketball was invented in 1891.

9 Origami
a   What is it?
b   T/F: The word *origami* comes from Chinese.

4 Pasta
a   What is it?
b   T/F: Pasta dates back to about 1000 BCE.

7 Boxing
a   What is it?
b   T/F: Boxing originated in England.

6 Square dancing
a   What is it?
b   T/F: Square dancing is American in origin.

5 Pilates
a   What is it?
b   T/F: Pilates developed in the eighteenth century.

4 ACADEMIC LISTENING AND NOTE TAKING: The Globalization of American Slang

In this section, you will hear and take notes on a two-part lecture by Cynthia Wiseman, a professor of English and linguistics (the study of language). The title of her lecture is *The Globalization of American Slang.* Professor Wiseman will discuss the growing popularity of American slang worldwide and explain how it spreads.

BEFORE THE LECTURE

BUILDING VOCABULARY

1 | How much American slang do you know? Take the following quiz to find out! Fill in each blank with the appropriate slang expression from the list below:

   1 If you like something, you can say it is _____awesome_____.

   2 This expression means "good-bye": _____

   3 Another word for "things": _____

   4 When you have no idea what is going on, you are _____.

   5 A term meaning "man": _____

   6 An expression meaning "calm down": _____

   7 If you are very tired, you are _____.

   8 An expression meaning "I don't mind" or "it doesn't matter": _____

   9 When you want to encourage someone, you can say: _____

   10 Something that is very important is _____.

awesome
beat
chill out
clueless
guy
a big deal
see ya
stuff
way to go
whatever

2 | Work in small groups and compare your answers. Then check your answers at the bottom of the page.

3 | As a class, discuss other American slang expressions that you know.

🎧 NOTE TAKING: LISTENING FOR RESTATEMENTS

> Lecturers often explain a concept they have just referred to using different words. In other words, they restate what they have said. Restatements are often, but not always, introduced with a signal phrase. Here is an example:
>
> signal phrase
>
> The focus of today's lecture is the globalization of American slang: in other words,
>
> restatement
>
> how American English slang is used by people all over the world.

1 Read these excerpts from the lecture. Work with a partner and discuss ways to complete the sentences by restating the items in italics.

1 Slang is, and I'm quoting a dictionary here, "a type of language used especially in speech among particular *speech communities*," that is, _____.

2 Slang is tremendously popular among young people because it's all about *"what's happening now."* That means _____.

3 This way of speaking is very attractive: it's creative and cool, as I mentioned, and it's very *youth-oriented,* meaning that _____.

4 Young people around the world hear *celebrities,* you know, _____, speaking or singing American slang.

5 In the last quarter century, this word *has invaded every corner of the English-speaking world.* . . . I mean, _____.

2 Listen to the excerpts and compare your responses with what the lecturer says.
▶ **PLAY**

LECTURE, PART ONE: What Is American Slang?

GUESSING VOCABULARY FROM CONTEXT

1 The following items contain important vocabulary from Part One of the lecture. Work with a partner. Using the context and your knowledge of related words, take turns trying to guess the meanings of the words in **bold**.

_____ **1** Now, as a professor of linguistics, I'm very interested in this **phenomenon**.

_____ **2** See what the **store owner** said?

_____ **3** In the second part, we'll look at how American slang seems to travel the globe so **effortlessly**.

_____ **4** Slang is **tremendously** popular among young people.

2 Work with your partner. Match the **bold** terms in the sentences in step 1 with their definitions below. If necessary, use a dictionary to check your answers.

a person who owns a shop or business   **c** fact, happening

b easily   **d** extremely, very

🎧 NOTE TAKING: COMBINING THE SKILLS

In this book, you have learned skills that can help you to take clear notes on lectures.

As you listen to a lecture, you have learned how to identify:

_____ ☐ The plan of the lecture
_____ ☐ Main ideas and supporting details
_____ ☐ Organizational phrases and signal words
_____ ☐ Key words

As you take notes, you have learned how to:

_____ ☐ Use symbols and abbreviations
_____ ☐ Use telegraphic language
_____ ☐ Use numbers and bullets
_____ ☐ Use handouts
_____ ☐ Record numerical information
_____ ☐ Organize your notes in an appropriate format, such as a chart, columns, a map, an outline, or a point-by-point format
_____ ☐ Write questions and comments about what you have heard

After you listen to a lecture, you have learned how to:

_____ ☐ Clarify things you do not understand
_____ ☐ Review your notes
_____ ☐ Use your notes to study for a test

As you continue to practice, you will find that you can combine all these note-taking skills whenever you take notes.

1 | Listen to Part One of the lecture and take notes. ▶ PLAY

2 | Write questions and comments about what you have heard and discuss them in a small group or as a class. Clarify anything you don't understand.

3 | Rewrite your notes neatly in the format you think would be best.

4 | In the list above, check (✔) the box next to each skill you practiced in taking notes for Part One of this lecture. Then evaluate your skills using arrows. Put one of the following arrows on the line next to each skill:

↑   made a lot of improvement
→   made some improvement
↓   need to improve more

LECTURE, PART TWO: Why American Slang Travels the Globe

GUESSING VOCABULARY FROM CONTEXT

1 The following items contain important vocabulary from Part Two of the lecture. Work with a partner. Using the context and your knowledge of related words, take turns trying to guess the meanings of the words in **bold**.

_____ **1** American slang is spread by music, TV, and movies, which are **gaining in** popularity all over the world.

_____ **2** TV allows American slang to spread **like wildfire**.

_____ **3** Listen to the following **segment**, recorded among American teenagers. . . .

_____ **4** Young people today are very **electronically literate**.

_____ **5** So, let's **wrap** this **up**.

_____ **6** And the Internet really **reinforces** the power of slang.

2 Work with your partner. Match the **bold** terms in the sentences with their definitions below. If necessary, use a dictionary to check your answers.

a end, conclude   **d** part (of a recording)
b makes stronger   **e** quickly
c becoming more and more   **f** used to technology

🎧 NOTE TAKING: COMBINING THE SKILLS

1 Listen to Part Two of the lecture and take notes on your own paper. ▶ **PLAY**

2 Reorganize and rewrite your notes as necessary to make them as clear as possible.

3 Exchange your notes with a partner. Use the checklist below to evaluate your partner's notes. Check (✔) the skills that your partner used.

> My partner . . .
> ☐ Has clear notes that are easy to read
> ☐ Has identified the main ideas and supporting details
> ☐ Has recorded numerical information correctly
> ☐ Has identified the key words
> ☐ Has used symbols and abbreviations
> ☐ Has used telegraphic language
> ☐ Has organized his or her notes in an appropriate format, such as a chart, columns, a map, an outline, or a point-by-point format
> ☐ Has written questions and comments about what he or she heard

4 Work with your partner and review your checklists. Discuss and correct any problems.

AFTER THE LECTURE

UNDERSTANDING HUMOR ABOUT THE TOPIC

Remember that if you can understand and appreciate humor about a topic, such as cartoons or jokes, it means that you have probably understood the main points of the topic.

1 Look at the three cartoons about American slang below and on the next page.

2 With a partner, take turns describing these cartoons.

3 Discuss the following questions about each cartoon with your partner:
   1 What is the main idea, or main point, of the cartoon?
   2 Why is it funny?

"No, no, no! You're, like, 'I really, really, really love you,' and you're, like, 'Whatever.'"

"This has merit, but could you go back through and add more 'like's and 'you know's?"

YOUR ENGLISH TEACHER SAYS YOU USE TOO MANY AMERICANISMS

WELL, LIKE, DUH! HE'S SO BLA BLA BLA DUDE

TEAM A, LOOK AT THESE ANSWERS:

Answers for Board A, page 150

1 Barbie dolls
  a best-selling American dolls since 1959
  b T: Barbie dolls are based on Lilli dolls, which were German.

2 Blue jeans
  a originally work pants that became popular around the world in the 1950s
  b F: The name comes from the French, *bleu de Gênes,* referring to the color.

3 Waltz
  a ballroom dance that became fashionable in the 1780s
  b F: The waltz originally came from Vienna, Austria.

4 Burrito
  a a Mexican dish made of a flour tortilla filled with meat or cheese
  b F: The word *burrito* is commonly used in English to refer to this dish.

5 Video games
  a games played on a video screen that involve an interaction between the games and the players
  b F: Video games were invented in the United States.

6 Reggae
  a a musical genre that developed in the 1960s
  b T

7 Soccer
  a a team sport played between two teams of 11 players each
  b F: FIFA, the International Association of soccer, is based in Switzerland.

8 Hollywood
  a refers to the American film and television industry
  b F: Hollywood is a district in Los Angeles.

9 Rap music
  a a style of music that first became popular in the 1980s
  b T

TEAM B, LOOK AT THESE ANSWERS:

Answers for Board B, page 151

1 Bollywood films
  a Hindi-language film industry in India
  b T

2 Feng shui
  a ancient practice of arrangement of space
  b F: Feng shui comes from China.

3 Handheld fans
  a accessories that are used to keep cool and look elegant
  b F: The earliest handheld fans came from Egypt.

4 Pasta
  a a type of food made from flour, water, and eggs
  b F: Pasta dates back to about 2000 BCE.

5 Pilates
  a a popular physical fitness system
  b F: Pilates developed in the twentieth century.

6 Square dancing
  a a folk dance in which four couples are in a square
  b F: Square dancing is very popular in the United States, but it probably originated in Europe in the seventeenth century.

7 Boxing
  a a sport where two players of similar weights fight together
  b F: Boxing probably existed in Africa as early as 4000 BCE.

8 Basketball
  a a sport in which two teams of five players try to score points by throwing a ball through a hoop
  b T

9 Origami
  a the art of paper folding
  b F: The word *origami* comes from Japanese.

CREDITS

Text Credits

Chapter 3

38 Pie charts based on information from *Historical Statistics of the United States, 2006*

Chapter 4

52 Pie charts based on information from *Statistical Yearbook of the Immigration and Naturalization Service, 2002.* Washington, D.C.; United States Government Printing Office

53 Excerpts from Public Agenda's survey, "Now That I'm Here." Used with permission.

Chapter 6

86 "Walls: A Poem for Tolerance," Pebbles Salas. Used with permission.

Photographic and illustration credits

1   © Bettmann/Corbis

2   © Courtesy of US Mint

3   © Courtesy of US Mint

4   © Jeff Greenberg/Alamy

15 *(left to right)* © Paul J. Richards/Getty Images; © Landov; © Brooks Kraft/Corbis

16 Library of Congress

33 © Shutterstock

34 © US Postal Service

41 *(left to right)* Library of Congress; © Fotosearch

47 © Bettmann/Corbis

50 © Bob Daemmrich/PhotoEdit

58 *(left to right)* © Clip Art.com; © Istock Photos; © Clip Art.com; © Clip Art.com

64 © Istock Photo

65 © Shutterstock

66 © The Bridgeman Art Library/Getty Images

67 Library of Congress

68 *(left to right)* © Punchstock; Library of Congress; © Hulton Archive/Getty Images

69 *(left to right)* © Corbis; © Bettmann/Corbis; Library of Congress

73 © Istock Photo

75 *(left to right)* Library of Congress; © Courtesy of National Women's History Museum

81 © Courtesy of BBC

84 *(bottom, clockwise from top left)* © Shutterstock; © Shutterstock; © Clip Art.com; © Shutterstock; © Hemera

87 © PhotoEdit

88 © Illustration by Paul Mudie, FAIR Multimedia

90 *(left to right)* © PhotoEdit; © Chuck Savage/Corbis; © Brian Bahr/Getty Images; © Jupiter Images

97 Library of Congress

98 © Jupiter Images

99 © Courtesy of Rochester Library

106 *(left to right)* © Sorbo Robert/Corbis; © Shutterstock; © Courtesy of DC Comics

110 *(left to right)* © Walt Disney Pictures/ Pixar Animation/Bureau L.A. Collection/ Corbis; © Courtesy of Denver Public Library

112 © John Henley/Corbis

113 *(all)* © Shutterstock

120 © PhotoEdit

122 *(both)* © Shutterstock

129 *(clockwise from top left)* © Shutterstock; © Istock Photos; © Shutterstock; © Clip Art.com; © Istock Photos; © Clip Art. com; © Shutterstock; © Shutterstock; © Istock Photos; © Clip Art.com; © Clip Art.com

130 *(all)* © Shutterstock

131 *(top row, all)* © Istock Photos; *(middle row, left to right)* © Shutterstock; Istock Photos; © Shutterstock; *(bottom row, left to right)* © Courtesy of Black and Decker; © Fotosearch; © Istock Photos

135 *(bottom, both)* © The Everett Collection

138 *(left to right)* © Tim Mosenfelder/Corbis; © Courtesy of Circle Player; © AP Wide World Photos; © AP Wide World Photos

144 © Shutterstock

145 *(clockwise from top left)* © Jochen Tack/ Alamy; © Earl & Nazima Kowall/Corbis; © Edd Westmacott/Alamy; © PhotoEdit

146 *(all)* © Clip Art.com

156 © CartoonBank

157 *(both)* © CartoonBank

Irene Williams

Cover: Gee's Bend Quilt by Irene Williams, image courtesy of Tinwood Media

Photo of Irene Williams by William Arnett, courtesy of Tinwood Media

The art on the cover of this book is a quilt by Irene Williams of Gee's Bend, Alabama. Gee's Bend is an African-American community whose women are famous for their original, hand-stitched quilts made of swatches of clothing and other textiles from everyday life. Gee's Bend quilts have been exhibited in museums around the United States; *The New York Times* said they are "some of the most miraculous works of modern art America has produced." For more information about the women of Gee's Bend and their quilts, go to http://www. quiltsofgeesbend.com

TASK INDEX

The skills taught and practiced in *Academic Listening Encounters: American Studies* and all *Academic Encounters* books help prepare students for the TOEFL® iBT exam.

Page numbers in boldface indicate tasks that are headed by commentary boxes.